101 Fun Activities to do in the Poconos

An Insider's Guide to Fun, Adventure, Thrills, and Chills in Pennsylvania's Vacationland

First Edition

Lauren E Robins

VORONA
PUBLISHING

101 Fun Activities to do in the Poconos

An Insider's Guide to Fun, Adventure, Thrills, and Chills in Pennsylvania's Vacationland

Lauren E Robins

ISBN:9798834877912

Cover design by: Rebecca Ira
Library of Congress Control Number: 2018675309
Printed in the United States of America

Contents

101 FUN ACTIVITIES
TO DO IN THE
POCONOS

MONROE COUNTY (1M-26M)

1M - Great Wolf Lodge
2M - Quiet Valley Historical Farm
3M - Frazetta Art Museum
4M - Antoine Dutot Museum & Gallery
5M - Pocono International Raceway
6M - Callie's Candy Kitchen
7M - Delaware Water Gap National Recreation Area
8M - Waterparks
9M - Mount Airy Casino Resort
10M - Pocono Music Festival (location varies by year)
11M - Fishing
12M - Golf
13M - Mountain Creek Riding Stables
14M - Kayaking, Canoeing, or Rafting on the Delaware
15M - Big Pocono State Park
16M - Stroud Mansion
17M - Bird Watching at Cherry Valley National Wildlife Refuge
18M - Antiquing
19M - Skiing
20M - Skytop
21M - Shopping at The Crossings Premium Outlets
22M - Arctic Paws Sled Dog Tours
23M - Air Tours: Moyer Aviation
24M - Cherry Valley Vineyards
25M - Klues Escape Room
26M - Schisler Museum of Wildlife & Natural History and McMunn Planetarium

CARBON COUNTY (52C-76C)

52C - Eckley's Miner's Village
53C - Lehigh Gorge Scenic Railway in Jim Thorpe
54C - Covered Bridges
55C - Oktoberfest at Blue Mountain Resort
56C - Skiing
57C - Mauch Chunk Lake Park
58C - Penn's Peak
59C - Beltzville State Park-Boating, Swimming, Volleyball, Soccer, Hiking, Waterfall
60C - Lehigh Gorge State Park
61C - Hickory Run State Park - Fishing, Waterfalls (Shades of Death), Prime Fall Foliage
62C - Adventure Center at Whitewater Challengers-Whitewater Rafting, Inflatable Kayaking, Camping
63C - Asa Packer Mansion Museum
64C - Old Jail Museum
65C - Bear Mountain Butterfly Sanctuary
66C - Shopping in Downtown Jim Thorpe
67C - The Mauch Chunk Opera House
68C - Mauch Chunk Museum and Cultural Center
69C - Pocono Whitewater - Pirate Rafting, Moonlight Rafting, Dam Release, Paintball
70C - Jim Thorpe Sidecar Tourz
71C - Broadway Grille - Live Music on Weekends
72C - Skirmish Paintball
73C - Stabin Museum and Cafe Arielle
74C - No9 Coal Mine and Museum
75C - Deer Path Riding Stables
76C - Fall Foliage Scenic Drive

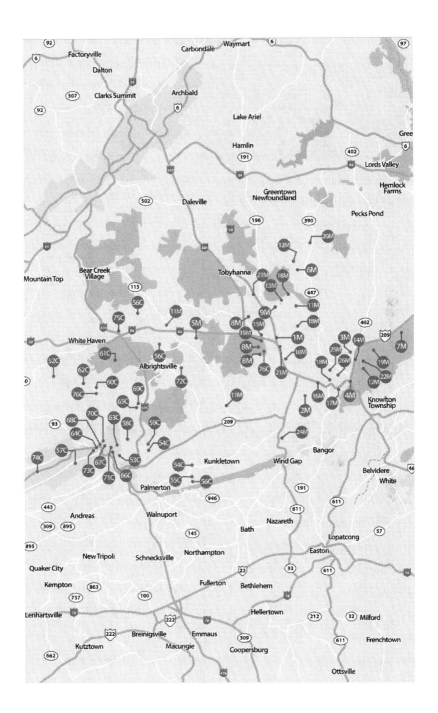

101 FUN ACTIVITIES
TO DO IN THE
POCONOS

PIKE COUNTY (27P-51P)

27P - Lackawaxen River Swimming Hole
28P - Hackers Falls
29P - Costa's Family Fun Park
30P - Bushkill Falls
31P - Woodloch
32P - Gray Towers National Historic Site + Town of Milford
33P - The Columns Museum
34P - Upper Delaware Scenic and Recreational River - Fishing
35P - The Upper Mill
36P - Golf: Paupack Hills
37P - Zane Gray Museum
38P - Pocono Environmental Education Center
39P - Hiking: Lower Hornbecks Creek Trail
40P - Eagle Watching
41P - Indian Head Canoes and Rafts
42P - Ski Big Bear at Masthope Mountain
43P - The Artery - Fine Art and Craft Gallery
44P - Raymondskill Falls
45P - Roebling Aqueduct
46P - Kittatinny
47P - Shohola Falls
48P - Dingman's and Silver Thread Falls
49P - Milford Beach
50P - Log Tavern Brewing
51P - The Artisan Exchange - American Fine Art and Gifts

WAYNE COUNTY (77W-101W)

77W - Wayne County Historical Society and Museum - Replica of First Steam Locomotive
78W - Pieces of the Past Antiques
79W - Lake Wallenpaupack (Scenic Boat Tour)
80W - Cross Current Guides Services and Outfitters
81W - Golf: Cricket Hill Golf Club
82W - D&H Trail- Hybrid and Mountain Biking, Equestrians, Runners, and Hikers
83W - Eagle Watch Bus tours - Delaware Highlands Conservancy
84W - Jam Room Brewing Company
85W - D&H Canal Park at Lock 31 + Towpath Trail
86W - Bethel School - A One - Room Schoolhouse
87W - The Settlers Inn
88W - Dorflinger Factory Museum
89W - Dorflinger Suydam Wildlife Sanctuary
90W - Lacawac Sanctuary
91W - Audubon Art and Craft Festival
92W - Maude Alley Shopping
93W - Old Stone Jail
94W - The Great Wall of Honesdale
95W - Stourbridge Line - Railroad Trip
96W - Soaring Eagle Rail Tours - Railbiking
97W - Harmony in the Woods
98W - Ritz Company Playhouse
99W - Penny Lane Candies and Candles
100W - Hawley Silk Mill
101W - Hawley Winterfest

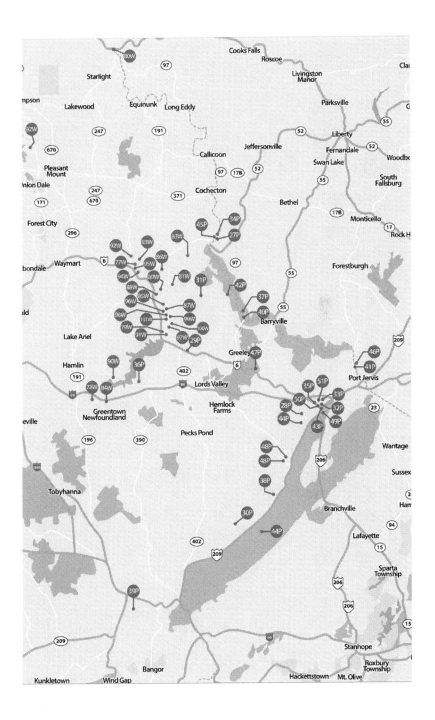

Introduction

"The mountains are calling and I
must go."

— John Muir

———

I am thrilled to write a book about my favorite place in the
world, the Pocono Mountains. I have been coming to the
Poconos to vacation since I was in my mother's womb. My
grandparents had a vacation house in Skytop, in Monroe
County. It was a beautiful big white house with black shut-
ters around gorgeous Skytop Lake, facing the magnificent
West Mountain. It was the original farmhouse when the
lake was pastureland. We would visit from Chicago every
summer for three weeks, and those three weeks were the
best times of my life. My aunt and uncle also had a house in
nearby Buck Hill Falls. When my grandparents died, no
one wanted the house or could afford to buy it, so it was
sold. I was devastated. The place of all my happy childhood

memories (being dramatic here) was no longer in the family. This is very unusual for houses around the lake-they usually stay in families for generations. After losing the home, my parents died a year apart a few years later. So, we would visit my Aunt Lois and Uncle Rob in their Buck Hill house for vacations, especially on the Fourth of July. Skytop still held a significant place in my heart, however. One day I approached the old house owners to tell them that if they were ever selling it, I would be interested in buying it. They told me they were tearing it down as the foundation was unsafe. I burst into tears in front of them. The dream of owning that house again and reliving the memories was gone forever. I continued spending vacation time with my aunt, uncle, and cousins in Buck Hill, which crept further into my heart. I would always peruse real estate when visiting or back home, but it didn't make sense to have a home in the Poconos as we lived in Texas at the time. Then in 2017, since family members who lived in Texas had moved away, we decided to move to Pennsylvania to be closer to family there and on the East coast. I searched Buck Hill real estate one day and came across one of the older homes (i.e., not a golf cottage) that reminded me so much of the Skytop house. It even had 70's floral wallpaper in the bedroom dressing room, just like the Skytop kitchen had! I convinced my husband that it was a good idea, and we drove up to look at it the following weekend. We also looked at two other houses, but nothing could compare with the charms and mountain views of what would become the Robin's Nest. We were finally homeowners in the Poconos! It wasn't Skytop, it was Buck Hill, and it was much better. When we moved in, we were placed with a buddy family who helped us make the wonderful friends we have today. My cousins recently bought a house in Buck Hill, so it's a family getaway for us. Because my husband and I can work from home, we can spend the entire summer in Buck Hill, enjoying our friends and the best the area offers.

This book offers 101 fun activities to do in the Pocono Mountains. It is divided into sections based on the four major counties comprising the Poconos: Monroe, Pike, Carbon, and Wayne. Since Buck Hill is in Monroe County, I will have done the most activities in that county. But plenty of us have traveled outside Monroe County to do various activities and have reported their findings. I hope you enjoy this book as much as your time in the Poconos. It truly is a one-of-a-kind place!

I do want to note that I have not included lodging or restaurants in the activities listed. I include food if there is an activity to do at the eatery, and I write about some lodging like camping options at state parks, etc. Perhaps a future book will encompass everything you need to plan your stay in the Poconos.

Chapter One

Monroe County

1. Great Wolf Lodge

1 Great Wolf Dr. Scotrun 18355 (800)768-9653

Great Wolf Lodge is a vast resort featuring a massive waterpark, several fun attractions outside of the water for the whole family to enjoy, and a neat place to stay while you do it all.

Waterpark:

-Fort Mackenzie is a four-story interactive treehouse with water toys and kid-activated splash features. It also includes my kid's favorite water park feature, a giant bucket that tips over, sending 500 gallons of water onto waiting children below (well, not directly down, that is a lot of water!) (Minimum height 42")

-Slap Tail Pond is an ocean-like wave pool five feet deep at the deepest point. Relax and pretend you are on a Caribbean vacation.

-Crooked Creek is a 3 ft deep lazy river. Grab a tube and let your cares float away!

-River Canyon Run is a twisty-turny water slide designed for the entire family. (Min. height 42")

-Alberta Falls is a four-story tandem tube water slide exhilarating fast with quick banking turns and steep pitches. (Min. height 42", Max weight single rider or in the rear of double tube 250 lb, Max weight combined for two riders 400 lb with the smaller rider in front)

-Whooping hollow is a toddler play pool featuring small water slides. (Max height 52", guests less than 48" or weak/non-swimmers should wear a life jacket)

-Totem towers are the water slides you use to escape Fort Mackenzie once you've reached the top.

-Coyote Cannon is a water slide that drops you 40 feet before sending you into a water jet-fueled vortex of chills and thrills. (Min height 42")

-Double Barrel Drop is the ultimate one-of-a-kind water slide featuring flashing LED lights, hair-raising twists and turns, barrel drops, and 450-degree spins. (Min height 48")

-Hydro Plunge is a water slide-hybrid rollercoaster where you ride a raft, are propelled up a steep height by a motorized track, and then are sent plunging down a 52-foot vertical drop. You will race through enclosed tubes and twisting curves. (min height48")

-Cub Paw Pool is a play area for kiddos featuring water cannons, geysers, small water slides, and colorful jet skis with zero-depth entry. The deepest part is 18" deep. (max height 52")

-Chinook Cove is an area for playing basketball, splashing, swimming, and having a ball (see what I did there?). The pool depth is four feet.

-Bigfoot pass is a set of large, floating lily pads that will test your kid's balance, swiftness, and athletic ability. And if they fall off? Splash! (Max weight 400 lb)

-North hot springs is an adults-only hot tub. Let your muscles relax, and your cares float away while the kiddos play. Age limit over 21

-South hot springs is the warming pool for the entire family. Soak in the warmth during a break or at the end of the day. (No unsupervised use by children)

Attractions

-MagiQuest is a live-action game where you go on magical quests throughout the lodge using your wand to help you along the way. You choose a wand, imbue it with magical powers, and start your quest. You will be journeying through the magical forest kingdom of Vellara to save the Sacred Trees-and the magic of the Evergreen- from a nefarious force. As you travel, you will help the Four Tribes, learn to cast potent Runes, mighty battle foes, and in the end, become a Master Magi! Also, there is a Mini Magi Mode for children under five, which is the same concept, just easier for them to play with and complete.

-Oliver's Mining Co. is a play-mining activity where kids get to pan and dig for glittering gemstones that they take home in a keepsake bag with a gemstone ID card and personalized labels.

-Ten Paw Alley is a bowling alley just the right size for the entire family to enjoy! Featuring shorter lanes and small balls, which make the game easier for little ones to play and eventually master. After all that water time, this makes a great way to spend time as a family together on land.

-Northern Lights Arcade features games, prizes, and excitement for all! Bring your little adrenaline junkie here to dry out and try their hand at winning some great prizes.

-Moonstone mine is an interactive mining experience

that features a tricky mirror maze that will have you in stitches trying to work your way out-just don't bang your head too hard! After all that fun, pan for gemstones at Oliver's Mining Co (see above).

-Howl at the Moon Glow Golf is an immersive black light mini-golf adventure that is nature-themed and full of vivacious life.

-Build-a-Bear Workshop is a store where your children can make their favorite Great Wolf Kids characters a reality by creating them as a stuffed animal. You can choose the type of animal, their outfits, vibrant costumes, and accessories, then watch as the staff fills your new friend with plush.

https://www.greatwolf.com/poconos

2. Quiet Valley Living Historical Farm

347 Quiet Valley Rd Stroudsburg 18360 (570)992-6161

Quiet Valley is one of my favorite places to visit because I am an old soul and one of the places we always bring out-of-town guests. It is a living history museum, and the workers/volunteers here make the farm come to life. They have accurately preserved the sights, sounds, and smells of a 19th-century Pennsylvania German Farmstead. They offer fun weekly events, from needle felting to hearth cooking workshops and everything farm or 19th century Pennsylvania. Even if you don't go to an event, there is still plenty to see and do. Interpreters are dressed in period clothing and portray the members of a German family who settled and lived here in the 18th and 19th centuries. You can see them perform tasks such as spinning and weaving in the cabin, hearth cooking and food preservation in the farmhouse, and animal husbandry in the barn. Group Tours are available by reservation. They feature premium activities such as a wagon ride through our covered bridge to see the heirloom apple orchard and pond, a tour of the kitchen gardens, or a visit to the one-room schoolhouse. The farm also hosts various festivals, such as the Farm Animal Frolic, Pocono State Craft Festival, Harvest Festival, Spooky Days on the Farm, or Old Time Christmas. I urge you to check out their website www.quietvalley.org to see what festivals may occur when you plan your trip. They also have the cutest little gift shop, and every time I go, I can't help but buy something for myself or a gift for someone else. Usually another Christmas ornament, I have a problem purchasing those, especially if they feature birds.

www.quietvalley.org

Image by klimkin from Pixabay

3. Art Museums: Frazetta Art Museum

141 Museum Rd East Stroudsburg 18301 (570)242-6180

Frazetta Art Museum contains the largest number of original works by Frank Frazetta in the world. The museum is run by the children and grandchild of Frank, who are more than willing to discuss the artist and the works or leave you alone to ponder their beauty and impact. The museum was opened by Frank's son Frank Jr in 2013 on the 67-acre estate where the family grew up, and the artist completed his original works. In addition to housing Frazetta's original oil pieces and countless pencil, pen, ink, and watercolor renderings, the museum also contains personal items such as part of Frazetta's camera collection, sports equipment, and art supplies like his easel, pallet, and more. Famous works here include Silver Warrior, Death Dealer III, The Indomitable, and Cat Girl. They have only sold original artwork twice: once to obtain the museum and once to keep it. That's not to say it will never happen again, but I wouldn't go counting on it. There is, however, an online store that benefits the museum.

http://frazettamuseum.com/

4. Antoine Dutot Museum & Gallery

24 Main Street (Rte 611) Delaware Water Gap 18327 (570)476-4240

This museum is housed in a charming brick schoolhouse circa 1850. It is named after Antoine Dutot, a settler who founded the town of Delaware Water Gap (originally called Dutotsburg) in 1793 and opened its first resort. This museum details the history of the town of Delaware Water Gap and how it went from a cozy mountain village to a first-rate resort town in the late 19th century. The spell-binding exhibits include Indian relics, resort memorabilia, Kentucky rifles, a drum from the War of 1812, and land deeds dating back to 1745. Also included are pictures of famous visitors such as Teddy Roosevelt and Fred Astaire. While watching a short film on the town's history, you sit in a 1930's era classroom. Then venture downstairs and view an exquisite art gallery with revolving exhibits of regional artists. The last stop is a separate building housing a restored 1926 American LaFrance fire engine, antique horse-drawn sleighs, and fire implements.

http://www.dutotmuseum.com/

5. Pocono Raceway

1234 Long Pond Rd, Long Pond 18334 1-800-RACEWAY

Pocono Raceway (formerly Pocono International Raceway) is a superspeedway known as the Tricky Triangle due to the unique shape of its track. Each turn is modeled after turns at different tracks. Turn One was modeled after the now out-of-commission Trenton Speedway. Turn Two (also known as the Tunnel Turn) is similar to the Indianapolis Motor Speedway. Turn three is akin to the Milwaukee Mile. The length (2.5 miles), the acute turns, and low banking tends to make speeds much lower overall than at other tracks of similar lengths. For this reason, restrictor plates are not needed here. Some refer to PR as a modified road course due to shifting gears to handle the range between the slowest curve and the fastest straightaway. This atypical design makes the set-up of the car and the crew's ability to make chassis adjustments even more essential here than at other tracks. It can spell a win or near-catastrophe. Drivers either love it or hate it. The bottom line is that the fans thoroughly enjoy spending the day at Pocono Raceway. Whether watching a Nascar Race, getting to do their own Stock Car Experience, or living the dream of driving an exotic car around the racetrack- no day is a waste when it's spent at Pocono Raceway. PR is home to the Pocono 400, a NASCAR Cup Series Race (160 laps/400 miles). Besides NASCAR races, PR is used by motorcycle and sports car clubs and racing schools throughout the year.

Why not catch the Air Show or a Music Festival if you're not into racing? Or simply join your race-crazy loved ones and camp at the racetrack while they enjoy the racing. The people-watching alone is sure to keep you entertained for hours.

See the website www.poconoraceway.com for the schedule of events.

6. Callie's Candy Kitchen

1111 PA-390, Mountainhome 18342 (570)595-2280

Callie's is a place so near and dear to my heart that, as a family, we named one of our current cats Callie in their honor. I have been going to Callie's to buy sweet treats since childhood. And not much has changed, which is just how I like it. One sad thing has changed, however. The owner, Mr. Callie, passed away in 2013 at the age of 80. Mr. Callie used to give rambunctious candy-making demonstrations in the candy "kitchen," which involved slapping various items into a tray of melted chocolate. He would ask the audience, "what do I make here at Callie's?" People would chime in "Candy" or "Chocolate." But those in the know knew the answer was "money." That brought a laugh. And you knew it wasn't true. No man in his 70's stood all day long with his hands in liquid chocolate entertaining guests because that was brought in the money. No, that was what brought Mr. Callie happiness. That's what Mr. Callie considered himself- a purveyor of joy. And that's what he has been since 1952. What started in Vermont in 1952, when Harry Callie bought his first shop, became what we know now in Monroe County as the only place to go for the best treats around 1972. Callie's has everything you could ever dream of in terms of candy, chocolate, and even treats for your pooch back home. There is a case full of truffles, chocolate-covered strawberries, and other delicious goodies when you enter. Go to your right, pass by the delicious homemade fudge in various flavors (my favorite is cookie dough), and enter lollipop land, featuring themed chocolate lollipops. Need a gift for your boss or teacher? They've got a lollipop for them. Need one in the shape of Dolly Parton? You're covered too. Head left from there and find all sorts of items, from chocolate-covered toffees and pretzels to chocolate-covered gummy bears.

Do yourself a favor and pick up a bag of the Pocono mints. They are a Pocono legend. They used to be served in a dish at the Skytop Lodge for guests to enjoy, but alas, that custom is a relic of the past. Move further inside, and there is a room your kiddos will enjoy with all types of candy, including some vintage treats and stuffed animals to delight your young ones. Keep going, and you will find more savory items like chocolate-covered popcorn. Dream it up, and they have covered it in chocolate to sell, even cream cheese! Then you finish your tour, probably laden with a ton of sweets, at the Candy Kitchen Museum where Mr. Callie used to give his talks. There is equipment to see and a bonus of a video of Mr. Callie giving one of his special talks so you can travel back in time and enjoy what I have for so many years. Before you check out, don't forget gifts for those back home. They will be incredibly jealous when they see all your purchased goodies. That's if they last that long! And if you are home again and find yourself craving something from Callie's, don't worry. They have an online store that ships straight to you. Just be aware that they won't ship chocolate in hot weather for obvious reasons. I truly hope you enjoy your visit to Callie's as I have for many years. www.calliescandy.com

My family and I outside Callie's in the fall

7. Delaware Water Gap National Recreation Area

1978 River Rd, Bushkill 18324 (570)426-2452

Get back to nature and visit this awe-inspiring park that has been treasured for over 12,000 years. It boasts 100+ miles of hiking trails, 40 miles of the Middle Delaware National Scenic and Recreational River, and three swim beaches where you can chill out and enjoy a picnic.

PICNIC AREAS in Pennsylvania

- Hialeah Picnic Area (Pets not permitted from Memorial Day to Labor Day weekends) (Closed to vehicle traffic Friday 8:00 pm to Monday noon May 21 to October 2)
- Smithfield Beach (Fee area; alcohol not permitted; pets not allowed from Memorial Day to Labor Day weekends)
- Milford Beach (Fee area; alcohol not permitted; pets not allowed from Memorial Day to Labor Day weekends; group picnic area available
- George W. Childs Park (Grills and pets not permitted)
- Tom's Creek
- Bushkill Village
- Hidden Lake
- Loch Lomond

Picnic Areas in New Jersey

- Kittatinny Point (Grills and alcohol are not permitted)
- Millbrook Village
- Turtle Beach (Fee area; alcohol and pets not permitted)
- Namanock
- Crater Lake (Grills are not permitted) (Closed to vehicle traffic Friday 8:00 pm to Monday noon May 21 to October 2)

Hiking

Delaware National Water Gap Recreational Area offers over 150 miles of hiking trails of varying difficulty to give you options to get out into nature and feel its healing effects. In the winter, it transforms, and cross-country skiing and snowshoeing become the major attractions. Whatever the season, please wear sturdy footwear made for hiking, bring enough water for all hikers, and remember to follow the seven principles of leaving no trace. Parking for the most popular trails like Mt. Tammany, Mt. Minsi, Raymondskill Falls, Dingmans Falls, Hackers Falls in Pennsylvania, and Buttermilk Falls in New Jersey, are usually full by 9:00 am on Saturdays and Sundays, from spring to fall. You can side-step crowded trailheads by hiking early on weekdays or choosing a less busy trail, such as Milford Knob Trail in Pennsylvania or Rattlesnake Swamp Trail in New Jersey. And don't let the intimidating name scare you. This trail is quiet and peaceful.

Visitors can opt to use a shuttle bus that allows you to park at the Pennsylvania Welcome Center or Delaware Water Gap Park and Ride and shuttle to the most popular trailheads without the parking hassles. New in 2022, there is a special hiker shuttle to increase weekend access to Raymondskill Falls. Guests can park at the North Contact Station/Milford Knob Trailhead parking and be shuttled to Raymondskill Falls. To view shuttle routes and schedule information, please visit the MCTA Hiker Shuttle website.

https://www.gomcta.com/trip.php

Historic Places

Delaware Water Gap National Recreation Area also contains several historic houses or villages (some containing museums) dating from the 1700 to 1800s for you to visit and venture back in time. They often include volunteers performing traditional work of the day. They include Millbrook Village, Foster Armstrong House & Neldon Roberts Stonehouse, Walden Center & Van Campen Inn, Village of Bevans(adapted as Peters Valley School of Craft), and Old Mine Road. See https://www.nps.gov/dewa/planyourvisit/historic-places.htm for more information on the historic sites in the recreation area.

Image from Stockvault

8. Waterparks

Aquatopia

193 Resort Dr, Tannersville 18372 (570) 629-1665

Considered the US's #1 Indoor waterpark, Aquatopia is covered with PA's largest Texlon roof, which allows the gorgeous sun to shine through while you splash and play. Waterslides include the newest Mountain Mayhem, a fully immersive experience with the guest choosing between four options that will awaken all five senses. Others include Constrictor (a 511ft ride with an aquatube that constricts to 54" and expands to 7 feet in the corners), Outa-space Race (fully enclosed body slide with twists, turns, and drops), Paradise Plunge (a 60ft vertical free-fall body slide), Skydive Plummet (a free-fall body slide with a 360-degree figure-eight loop), Storm Chaser (North America's longest uphill water coaster with five gravity-defying drops), the

Himalayan (the only indoor head first mat waterslide in the region) and Venus Slydetrap (a 608 ft ride allowing 3-6 people per raft, the only combo raft ride of its kind). There is also a basketball lagoon, an area for stand-up or boogie boarding lessons on their 40,000 gallon/min flow surfing simulator, two play structures, a children's play area called Penguin Play Bay, an indoor/outdoor warm spa lagoon with hydrotherapy jets, the Great Ka-Na-Gawa Wavepool featuring the largest waves in the Northeast, and rounded out by a lazy river. Indoor activities include laser tag, rock climbing, an escape room, arcade, virtual reality, an indoor ropes course, bumper cars, and two stores for shopping offering souvenirs, sweet treats, or items left behind at home. You can visit for the day or stay at one of the 453 hotel guest suites.

https://www.camelbackresort.com/waterparks/ poconos-pa-indoor-water-park/

Camelbeach

301 Resort Dr, Tannersville 18372 (570)629-1661

Waterslides include the Checkered Flag Challenge (getting an upgrade for the 2022 season), Dune Runner (featuring quad tubes and triple dune drops that gather speed before dropping you into the pool below), High Noon Typhoon (six-story funnel which gives you a weightless feeling as you soar above the treetops in quad tubes), Sand Storm (quad tube with two tantrum funnels), The Spin Cycle (the tube slide portion of the only pair of bowl slides in the Northeast USA), Titan (8 stories tall and nearly three football fields in length it is the largest waterslide of its kind), Triple Venom (3 unique six-story body slides, Cobra, Viper, and Serpent with twists, turns, and drops), Tube

Slides (Sidewinder, Riptide, Twister, and Midnight Run featuring twists, turns and drops through the darkness), Vortex (the body slide portion of the only pair of bowl slides in the Northeastern US)

There is Kahuna Lagoon Wavepool that features waves of varying height up to the "Big Kahuna" size waves of 4-6 feet in height! Currently the largest waves in the Northeastern United States. Mummy's Oasis is a children's splash and play area featuring slides, sprinklers, water cannons, geysers, and a massive water bucket that dumps on playing children below (camel kids only). In addition, there is Pharaoh's Phortress, a family play structure with eight waterslides, a four-story tipping water bucket, fountains, and spray guns. On their surfing simulator, you can also try your hand at Flowriding or boogie boarding. Take the Blue Nile Adventure River, a 1000ft long lazy river journey complete with waterfalls, geysers, and bubbling waters if you're not into thrills.

https://www.camelbackresort.com/waterparks/
poconos-pa-outdoor-water-park/

Kalahari

250 Kalahari Blvd, Pocono Manor 18349

At 22,000 sq ft of African-themed, watery, fun, Kalahari waterpark is the largest indoor waterpark in Pennsylvania, and up until recently, it was the largest in the US. Waterslides include: the Anaconda (a family raft ride featuring sharp turns and high speed plunges), Barrelling Baboon (a guessing game of a ride leaves you wondering whether you will dip or twist as you enter the oscillating funnel), Cheetah Race (this mat slide allows you to race three friends), Elephant Trunk (a twisty-turny 270ft tandem tube slide), Kenya Korkscrew (twist and turn as you spiral down this tandem tube ride), Rippling Rhino (allows groups of 2-3 to navigate through a giant flume and encounter turns and drops before ending up in the catch pool), Sahara Sidewinders (features a nearly vertical plummet on a 250 ft journey that takes you through a gravity-defying 360 degree loop-de-loop before you splash down in the pool below), Screaming Hyena (for brave thrill seekers, this ride starts through the ROOF 60 feet above the water park floor!), Tanzanian Twister (Round and round you go in this funnel flume at up to 40 miles per hour then free fall into the 7 foot catch pool below), The Smoke that Thunders (named after Victoria Falls in Africa, this is a massive family raft ride), Victoria Falls (join the family on this 504 ft raft ride), Wild Wildebeest (you'll have to ride this one to find out how wet and wild it really is!), Zig Zag Zebra (like the name implies this tandem tube ride zigs and zags to rider to great delight), Zimbabwe Zipper (thrill seekers will enjoy this flume ride that sends you along at speeds up to 40 mph). Kalahari also features two children's play areas, a Flowrider, a 5 ft wave simulator, indoor and outdoor spas, a lazy river, a basketball lagoon, two swim-up bars, and a family play area with a water tipping bucket, and a wave pool. An outdoor section to Kalahari also features a bug-themed set of water slides and a large outdoor pool and sundeck. Kalahari also features an outdoor mini-golf course, a ropes course, a monkey climb for youngsters, and quad racing zip lines so you can race your family members to the finish line. Other indoor attractions include a large arcade, black light minigolf, VR, escape rooms, mini bowling, and a 7-D motion theater. Also at Kalahari is a full spa with packages for teens and kiddos as young as 5 to join mommy or daddy on a spa day, several retail stores, and dining options.

https://www.kalahariresorts.com/pennsylvania/

9. Mount Airy Casino Resort

312 Woodland Rd, Mount Pocono 18344 1877-682-4791

I admit gambling at Mount Airy Casino is one of my secret vices. I love to gamble, especially blackjack or poker. Mount Airy is a large, beautiful casino with many tables for you to play all day or night. Dealers are friendly and skilled. A Starbucks in the lobby below keeps you fueled with the good stuff and free drinks while you play. My husband and I have had dinner there on several occasions and have been very happy with what we ordered, buffet and sit-down restaurants. Of course, Mount Airy offers top-notch resort rooms with pillow-top beds, spacious bathrooms, room service, WiFi, and much more for out-of-towners. I only wish I didn't have a house ten minutes away or I could justify staying there. Maybe I'll become a high roller one day, and they will comp me a room!

Mount Airy Casino Resort was the first casino resort in Pennsylvania to earn the prestigious AAA Four Diamond Rating and continues to keep that status more than a decade later. In terms of dining, they have a buffet, Guy Fieri's Mt. Pocono Kitchen, Bistecca by Il Mulino, Lucky 8 Noodle and Sushi Bar, Pizzeria Montagna, and a general snack and alcohol store called Last Call (how cute is that?). The other big draw to Mount Airy is the golf course. Designed by architect Hal Purdy after Sports Illustrated's "The Best 18 Golf Holes in America", each hole is modeled after golf's most legendary holes from Championship courses throughout the United States. The result is over 6,500 yards of stunning fairways, a picturesque view, and outstanding golf course conditions expected at private country clubs. Certified in 2018 by Audubon International, Mount Airy's Golf Course is a steward of environmental sustainability, protecting our environment while preserving the natural heritage of golf. This is something that I am thrilled to see, being an environmentalist myself. After a round of golf or many hands of blackjack, why not spend some relaxation time at the pool and spa. The spa offers Bamboo Massage, something I am eager to try this summer! Just have to earn the cost at the blackjack table, haha.

https://mountairycasino.com/

Image from Stockvault

10. Pocono Mountains Music Festival

THE POCONO MOUNTAINS MUSIC FESTIVAL was founded in 2009 as the Buck Hill Skytop Music Festival to offer musical and educational programming as a unique cultural resource for the Northeast Pennsylvania region. The festival highlights seasoned and up-and-coming performers in the disciplines, including cabaret, jazz, dance, chamber music, pop, country, and musical theater. The venues are cozy, allowing audiences unparalleled access to world-renowned musicians. The festival's noteworthy educational programming offers local students the opportunity to study and perform with music and theater professionals. The festival is something I have been meaning to get to since we moved here, but Covid and other life events have gotten in the way. My Aunt Lois and Uncle Rob, who also have a house in Buck Hill, have gone to many concerts at the Festival and have had a thoroughly good time.

https://www.poconofest.org/

11. Fishing

Paradise Brook Trout Company

123 Hatchery Drive, Cresco 18326 Fishing Preserve (570)629-0422

Paradise Brook Trout Company was founded in 1901 as a fish hatchery and raised fish continuously for over 100 years. The fishing preserve at Paradise Brook Trout Co. is located at the historic hatchery. They offer fishing for trout and bass in the idyllic setting of Paradise Valley. Any fish you catch must be paid for, but they will filet them for you and send you home with your catch so you can make a healthy, delicious meal. If you aren't into fishing, you can take a baggie of food, stroll along the hatchery, and feed the trout. The best part is that a license isn't required to fish here. It's the perfect spot for first-time anglers. Amenities include picnic tables, snacks and beverages, bathrooms, pole rentals, bait and tackle, and fish cleaning. Rules: no throwing fish back, no use of minnows or stringers, no pets, no entering the water, and no barbecuing.

I am an angler, and I usually fly fish in the streams at Buck Hill, but the history of this place makes me want to visit and fish. I wasn't aware that celebrities like Babe Ruth used to visit here and that their trout eggs were once so popular that they were shipped internationally. How neat!

https://paradisetrout.com/

Big Brown Fish and Pay Lakes

2668 Route 115, Effort 18330 (570)629-0427

In 1971 Charles A. Conklin II dammed a stream and dug a pond filling it with fish. He named many of the most distinctive fish, and his favorite was a fish called "Big Brown." Not long after this, the first fish was sold. When the hatchery became an actual business in 1984, Charles named it after "Big Brown." The hatchery produces 300,000 lb of Rainbow, Brown, Brook, and Golden Rainbow Trout and approximately 20,000 lb of Largemouth bass and Bluegill each year. Roughly 25% of the hatchery's fish are stocked in the fish and pay lakes, 65% are sold to private sport fishing, and 10% are sold to food processors.

Big Brown Fish and Pay Lakes has two fishing ponds for trout and one for largemouth bass. It is continually stocked with thousands of 12-20"+ trout from its hatchery. No fishing license is required. How fast will you catch fish? Well, that depends. An experienced angler will catch fish quickly, especially with moving lures. Someone without experience will take a little longer to learn the ropes. But once you get a feel for it, you will reel them in in two shakes of a lamb's tail! Weather is always a factor when fishing. Since bass prefer warmer water, they will bite more in the mornings of the summer months. Trout prefer colder water, but since there is a constant supply of cold water to the ponds, they continue to bite even on the hottest days.

How it works for fishing:

- There is no limit on the number of fish you can catch
- You must keep and pay for everything you catch
- A complete cleaning station is where staff gut and filet your fish for you.
- You may either rent poles there or bring your own to use
- There are picnic tables around the pond for use
- Rules: No throwing fish back-you must keep and pay for everything you catch.
- No pets allowed.
- No barbecuing.
- Stringers and minnows are not permitted.
- No entering the water.
- Fish must be brought up to the cleaning table 30 minutes before closing time

https://bigbrownfish.com/

Image by egustavogo from Pixabay

Austin T Blakeslee Recreation

Where: Near Blakeslee, Pa. Take Route 80 to Exit 284 – Route 115 North. After the Tobyhanna Creek bridge, parking areas are on the left. Note: Two trailheads serve Austin T. Blakeslee Natural Area.

GPS coordinates 41° 4' 59"N 75° 35' 4" W, elevation 1,560 feet.

This recreation area offers hiking, a waterfall, picnicking, fishing in season with a license, and other recreational activities. Picnic tables, barbecues, a covered pavilion, an information kiosk, and a port-a-potty at the lower trailhead. Motorized vehicles such as ATVs are allowed. Leashed dogs are welcome as long as owners clean up after them. The history of this area started in the 1930s when it was called Harrison Park, then later Toby Park. It contained a roller rink, dance hall, swimming pools, steam-operated carousel, penny arcade, and softball fields. Unfortunately, the Flood of 1955 wiped everything off the face of the earth. What an incredible loss! The ruins left behind are low walls and people's memories of fun times. In happier news, this area is now a 130-acre nature preserve. Several paths take you to the creek's edge where you can fish, spring through fall. Well-worn paths take you to the brink of the creek, where you are likely to find people fishing, spring through fall.

https://brodheadwatershed.org/austin-t-blakeslee-natural-area/

12. Golf

Buck Hill Golf Club

357 Golf Dr, Buck Hill Falls, PA 18323 (570)595-7730

Buck Hill Golf Club features 18 holes by Donald Ross and nine holes by Robert White, two Scotsman famous for golf course design. Robert White is recognized as one of the forefathers of golf in America, being one of the first designers and manufacturers of golf clubs in the USA. A groundbreaker, he was the first to build a putting green on the White House lawn. He has designed and built over 100 courses in his lifetime. At Buck Hill Golf Course, metal spikes are NOT permitted, credit cards are accepted, carts and clubs can be rented separately, a fully equipped pro-shop on-site, and a driving range and putting green. Lessons are available upon request. Having taken lessons here, I can tell you they are beneficial!

https://www.buckhillfalls.com/public/golf

Image by Megan Rodgers

The Shawnee Inn and Golf Resort

100 Shawnee Inn Drive, Shawnee on Delaware 18356
(800)742-9633

With 24 of 27 holes located on an island in the middle of the Delaware River, this championship golf course is truly picturesque and isolated from the outside world and its distractions. A uniquely flat course, the Shawnee Island Course is located on the grounds of the Shawnee Inn and was built in 1910 by A. W. Tillinghast, a member of the World Golf Hall of Fame. It has the distinction of being the first golf course he ever designed. Shawnee offers lessons for adults as well as children. Junior golfers play free with a paying adult as well. Also available for use at Shawnee Inn and Golf Resort is a 6-hole par 3 Chip n' Putt designed by Tom Doak. There is also a 250-yard-long driving range to practice before hitting the links. Before, during, or after your round(s), grab a drink or light snack at the Halfway

House. Their golf shop boasts anything you need to play the game. Shawnee requires 'Resort Attire' while on the golf course, consisting of pants, shorts, skirts, and collared shirts. No denim, cut-offs, t-shirts, or tank tops will be allowed. https://www.shawneeinn.com/poconos-golf-courses/

Image by Stefan Waldvogel from Pixabay

13. Mountain Creek Riding Stables

6190 Paradise Valley Rd, Cresco 18326 (570)839-8725

Mountain Creek has been in business for over 20 years, and while it started small, they have grown to become one of the best riding stables in the Poconos. Their strength is beginner and intermediate horseback riding on meandering trails through the woods. No experience is required to ride; their helpful and professional guides will choose the perfect horse to lead you on your journey. They are open seven days a week, rain or shine, all year long, and offer group trail rides, private trail rides, pony rides for little ones not old enough to ride a horse yet, wagon rides for the whole family, and carriage rentals for special events. Prices are very fair for what you are getting.

What To Expect

- Children must be at least seven years old and 50" tall to ride on a trail.
- Arrive 15-30 minutes before the scheduled time of your ride so you can fill out paperwork and get fitted for a helmet.
- Helmets are required for minors (anyone under 18). They provide helmets free of charge for any rider.
- Please wear secure shoes, no sandals or flip-flops. Boots with a short heel (1 to 1.5 inches ideally) or sturdy closed-toed shoes are recommended.
- Wear comfortable pants, so you do not get rubbing or blisters from the saddle.
- The weight limit is 240 pounds, though this depends on height. If anyone in your party is close to or over 240 pounds, please get their exact height and weight and give them a call or send an email and they will see if they have a horse that can accommodate them.
- They also have a minimum height requirement of 50" for adults and children.
- Children must be at least seven years old to ride.

https://mtcreekstable.com/

Image from Danni R from Pixabay

14. Kayaking, Canoeing, or Rafting on the Delaware River: Adventure Sports

Adventure sports

398 Seven Bridge Road, East Stroudsburg 18301 (570)223-0505 or (800)487-2628

Adventure Sports is licensed by the National Park Service and has been running trips on the Delaware River since 1969. Their specialty is kayak, river, and canoe trips down the beautiful Delaware River. They offer trips of varying distances from 2 hours to overnight to multi-day camping trips. They only use high-quality Old Town canoes and kayaks and Hyside rafts. I have been on several trips with Adventure Sports, but my favorite was a kayaking trip with my brother, John, in a tandem kayak and my husband in tandem with my eldest daughter, Genevieve. We laughed, swam in the river, and just had a blast. The trip we took was from Smithfield Beach to Delaware Water Gap, one of three featured trips they offer. I will mention details about these three featured trips but know many more trips are listed on their website.

Canoe, Kayak, or Raft from Smithfield Beach to Delaware Water Gap

This is one of their shorter trips down the Delaware River. But just because this trip is shorter doesn't mean it's any less beautiful or fun. You start your journey by taking a canoe, kayak, or raft from Smithfield Beach in East Stroudsburg, PA. This recreation area is a great spot to enjoy a picnic, relax on the grassy beach, or even go for a swim.

Once you put in at Smithfield Beach, you're in for an enjoyable and scenic float to the Delaware Water Gap. You'll pass many islands within the river, like Tocks, Labar, Depue, and Shawnee. Keep an eye out for wildlife like deer, bears, bald eagles, and more. Enjoy mountain views and the sensation of gently flowing water beneath you.

After six miles of canoeing, kayaking, or rafting, you reach the famous Delaware Water Gap, once considered a scenic Wonder of the World. This trip does not feature any difficult features or rapids and is suited for beginners so that the whole family can enjoy this fun Poconos kayaking, canoeing, or rafting adventure.

. . .

Canoe or Kayak the Delaware River from Bushkill to Smithfield Beach

Join Adventure Sports for a beautiful day trip down the Delaware River from the Bushkill boat launch in Lehman Township, PA, to Smithfield Beach in Stroudsburg, PA. You'll pass many scenic spots during your river trip, including the 'jumping rock' on the river's right-hand (Pennsylvania) side. You'll also pass Sambo Island and Poxano Island during your Poconos canoeing or kayaking trip.

Take in the natural beauty surrounding you as you enjoy a peaceful float to Smithfield Beach, where a grassy beach, picnic area, and swimming spots await you. You might see bald eagles, deer, bears, and other local wildlife along the riverbanks.

This trip does not feature any difficult features or rapids and is suited for beginners and people of all ages or experience levels.

Canoe or Kayak Bushkill to Delaware Water Gap

This is a beautiful one-day trip down the Delaware River from the Bushkill boat launch in Lehman Township, PA, to the Delaware Water Gap, PA.

As you paddle, keep an eye out for local wildlife like deer, bears, bald eagles, etc. Your trip takes you past many points of interest along the river, including the Historic Shawnee Inn, a gorgeous riverside resort whose roots date back to the 1890s.

You can also see the remains of the Old Karamac Resort and train crossing as you float toward the Delaware Water

Gap. And again, you will see the 'jumping rock,' located on the river's Pennsylvania side (right-hand side).

This trip does not feature any difficult features or rapids. Still, please be aware that six hours of paddling can be strenuous, so this trip is generally popular with more experienced paddlers. Spring and fall (when the water is higher) are the best seasons to enjoy this fantastic paddle, but you're in for a great time no matter when you visit!

They accept cancellations 24 hours before your trip with no penalty. You may also cancel on the day of your trip for bad weather at their location. Cancellations made the same day (before your reservation time) that are not because of the weather are subject to a cancellation fee of $15 per person per day. If you do not show up and do not call, you will be charged the whole rate-so make sure to call and cancel.

Make sure to wear appropriate clothing for the weather, bring a dry change of clothes, sneakers or river shoes, sun protection, hat, bathing suit & towel, packed lunch (or buy it there), cameras, binoculars, goggles, snorkel, or anything else you think you would need for a day on the river. Anyone over the age of two is welcome on river trips, but they must be able to swim. Fishing is allowed if you are over 16 years old and have a PA or NJ fishing license (they do not sell fishing licenses). Alcohol is permitted but not encouraged. National Park Rangers suggest a limit of three 12 oz. cans of beer per person per day. If you appear intoxicated, you are subject to arrest and removal from the river by the National Park Rangers. NO glass containers are allowed. Dogs are permitted in kayaks and canoes. They will transport them to the start, but if you do not finish where your vehicle is, they will not transport your dog back to your car after the trip due to your dog being wet and smelly (sorry, but true).

www.adventuresport.com

Image by Daina Krumins from Pixabay

15. Big Pocono State Park

CAMELBACK RD, Tannersville 18372 (570) 894-8336

The entrance to the park is from PA 715 and Exit 299 of I-80 at Tannersville. Use caution: there are steep grades, and visitors should not attempt this drive in vehicles with trailers in tow.

The park consists of 1,306 acres of craggy topography on Camelback Mountain and offers stunning vistas of three states. The park closes in early December and re-opens from sunrise to sunset the first week in April. Be aware that the roads may be closed in the winter due to snow. The best thing to do in this park is hike to the summit for the glorious view. From the summit, you can see Eastern Pennsylvania and portions of New York and New Jersey. If the day is particularly clear, you can see 100 miles to the Catskills. Also visible are Delaware Water Gap, Wind Gap, and Lehigh Gap. There is also a restaurant at the top of the summit called the Summit House, which offers fare such as fried chicken, burgers, and cocktails. Other activities to do in Big Pocono are mountain biking and picnicking.

https://www.dcnr.pa.gov/StateParks/FindAPark/ BigPoconoStatePark/Pages/default.aspx

https://poconogo.com/park-preserve/big-pocono-state-park/

16. Stroud Mansion Museum and Library and Shopping in Stroudsburg

900 Main Street, Stroudsburg 18360 (570)421-7703

Stroud Mansion is a stately home built in 1795 by Jacob Stroud, the founder of Stroudsburg and Revolutionary War Colonel. It is the finest example of Georgian architecture in Monroe County. It houses a museum dedicated to preserving the history of Monroe County and educating the public so it is not forgotten. There are four floors of exhibits to peruse that feature Monroe County history. Exhibits include artifacts from the time of the Native Americans to modern times. Rooms of note are an antique toy room, the early 18th century Stroud Room, an Authentic Colonial-era cellar kitchen, and a tool and weapons room.

Stroudsburg

Before or after you visit Stroud Mansion, take some time in Stroudsburg. There is so much they have to offer. From shopping at boutiques, browsing art galleries, attending a concert or play, or maybe timing it right to hit up the farmer's market, you can easily spend the entire day here.

https://www.monroehistorical.org/mansion.html
https://www.visitdowntownstroudsburg.com/

17. Bird Watching at Cherry Valley National Wildlife Refuge

2138 Croasdale Road, Stroudsburg 18360 (973)702-7266

Cherry Valley NWR is land especially preserved for migratory birds and their essential habitats. Five federally listed or endangered species make this land their home. The Kittatinny Ridge has been named an Important Bird Area by the National Audubon Society due to the sheer amount of migratory birds that pass through there (approx. 20,000 raptors and 140 other bird species every fall). If you're lucky, you can catch glimpses of warblers, wild turkeys, and bald eagles. Due to birds and the nature of birdwatching, no pets are allowed in the refuge. Please also remain on the trails at all times to protect the essential habitat and native flora.

https://www.fws.gov/refuge/cherry-valley

Image by Anelka from Pixabay

18. Antiquing in Monroe County

Antiquing is one of my favorite activities, and I have shopped in all the listed stores multiple times over the years. These are the best of the best. They all are a bit different, but all have unique items. You have to hunt for your treasures in some stores, and others are more on display.

Pocono Peddler's Village Antique Mall

246 Stadden Rd, Tannersville 18372 (570)629-6366
    Peddler's Village is a vast store with multiple stalls filled

with items that will evoke memories of the past and make you nostalgic. I found a set of red apple canisters in near-perfect condition that were precisely the ones my late grandmother used to have. I couldn't have picked them up fast enough! And the prices are very reasonable, and negotiations are always welcome here. They have something for everyone, from antiques like furniture and glassware to baseball cards, paintings, and vinyl records.

https://pocono-antiquemall.com/

Olde Engine Works

62 N 3rd Street, Stroudsburg 18360 (570)421-4340

I have to admit this is my favorite of all the stores listed. At 22,000 square feet with 100 unique vendors, there are endless antique and vintage goodies to peruse and buy. I bought my gorgeous Civil War-era round table with beautiful hand-carved twisted legs here. But I have also purchased a fur beret, a set of vintage board games, or an antique ring. There is such variety in this place and all quality items. This store is just off Main Street in Stroudsburg, so if you are visiting the Stroud Mansion or just spending the day in Stroudsburg shopping and visiting art museums, stop here and find yourself a treasure to remember your trip.

https://www.oldeengineworks.com/

Backroads Antiques

3424 Route 715, Henryville 18332 (570)872-9990

This is a much smaller shop but is chock-a-block with antiques and vintage items. They have big-ticket items like an old jukebox and an antique Pepsi machine. I bought some vintage flies for fly fishing there. Who knew you could buy something like that at an antique store? This place is almost like a museum with many incredible artifacts of the past. I remember seeing an old radio and noticing it had a channel for the Vatican. Interesting huh? This place is a little out of the way, depending on where you are traveling, but you won't regret coming here.

https://www.discovernepa.com/thing-to-do/backroads-antiques/

Barn Door Antiques

340 Route 390, Cresco 18326 (570)595-3418

I would say this is more of a "grown-up" antique shop. You don't have to do any hunting. Everything is laid out for you to see. Prices are higher, but the items are all very high quality. I got a favorite framed lithograph of two dogs that hangs in my dining room in Buck Hill and a colored pyrex mixing bowl set that matched one I had of my grandmother's but was missing two bowls, and I had broken the last one. To have that complete set meant everything to me! They have been voted one of the best antique shops in the Pocono Mountains. Their days and times vary by season, so check the website before making an itinerary.

http://www.barndoorantiques.com/

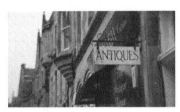

Image by Aly Ko

19. Skiing in Monroe County

Camelback Resort

301 Resort Drive, Tannersville 18372 (815)515-1283
According to their website, Camelback Resort has been named the #1 skiing destination in Pennsylvania. They offer skiing, snowboarding, tubing, and night skiing. They have the biggest snow tubing park in the region with 42 lanes to tube in, 39 skiing/snowboarding trails, and three ski-in/ski-out restaurants. This is a very popular resort and can get busy at times.

https://www.camelbackresort.com/

Shawnee Mountain

401 Hollow Road, East Stroudsburg 18301 (570)421-7231
Snow Report: 800-233-4218
Shawnee offers 23 trails for skiing and snowboarding with 25% beginner, 50% intermediate, and 25% expert. They also feature two terrain parks and a snow tubing slope. Lifts include 1 High-Speed Detachable Quad, 1 Fixed-Grip Quad, 4 Double, and 4 Carpets. The snow tubing park has up to 6 chutes with two carpets to get you up the slope.

https://www.shawneemt.com/mountain/

Image by Josef Pichler from Pixabay

20. Skytop

One Skytop Lodge Road, Skytop 18357 (855)345-7759

If you read the introduction, you know that Skytop is an extraordinary and significant place to me. Skytop offers so many things to do! And while it has always been my dream to stay in the lodge, you don't have to be a guest of the Lodge to enjoy most of the activities offered. The things off the list for non-staying guests are the swimming pools, the hiking trails, and the beach area. This is especially sad for me as I got engaged on top of West Mountain and can no longer visit the spot (unless I feel like being an outlaw, hehe). When you visit Skytop, if you're a thrill-seeker, you can visit the Adventure Center, which offers a tree ropes course, archery tag (best described as dodgeball with bows and arrows), paintball, and skiing or snow tubing in the winter. One of my favorite activities is to take a boat out on Skytop Lake. It's a relatively small lake, but it's beautiful and peaceful with the mountain overlooking the lake. You can take a kayak or canoe, and you may also fish on the lake. (Note that their website says this is for resort guests, but I have done this many times. I called and asked specifically what was available to non-staying guests, and they told me the only things off limits were what is listed above.) They also have paddle tennis, a gorgeous golf course, lawn bowling, tennis, biking, ice skating, and shooting. Ice skating is a favorite of my family. That rink is where my daughters and I learned to skate.

The Lodge itself is gorgeous and worth wandering around. Make your way up to the observation deck at the tip-top of the lodge for stunning panoramic views of the region. In the basement is an arcade my family has spent many hours playing in. In that area is a small food shop where you can get sandwiches, old-fashioned egg creams, and delicious ice cream sundaes. My mom always used to get the "Dusty Road," which has malted milk topping. The Lodge has several dining options, but our family's favorite is The Taproom. It is relaxed casual dining with delicious American cuisine. On certain nights the Lodge offers Bingo which is another favorite of mine. Call and check the schedule of the week's activities.

https://www.skytop.com/

Image by Beth Goldwater

21. Shopping at The Crossings Premium Outlets

1000 Premium Outlets Dr, Tannersville 18372

Outlet Management and Shopping Line (570)629-4650

Outlet Security (570)269-2970

The Crossings is somewhere I have spent a lot of time shopping. From when I was doing my back-to-school shopping every year to now getting my kids clothes, to just fun everyday shopping. The Crossings boasts over 100 brand name and designer stores, so there is something for everyone. From Polo Ralph Lauren to Coach, I love shopping at this outdoor mall. There are also multiple places to eat while shopping, such as Barley Creek Tasting Room & Pub, Johnny Rockets, and Crepe Soleil. And bonus: everything you buy is tax-free.

https://www.premiumoutlets.com/outlet/the-crossings

Image by StockSnap from Pixabay

22. Arctic Paws Sled Dog Tours

100 Shawnee Inn Drive, East Stroudsburg 18302 dogsled
tour@yahoo.com

At Shawnee Inn and Golf Resort, Arctic Paws offers
sled dog tours with or without snow. When there is no
snow, tours are with UTVs, and when there is a foot of
snow or more, the dog sled team uses actual sleds. The
website and reviews lead me to recommend this activity
only if there is sufficient snow for a snow tour. Tours are
restricted to anyone under ten years of age, those with
mobility issues, those unable to follow directions quickly,
and anyone with health concerns. Guests get to be
educated about huskies, get covered in doggie kisses, and
enjoy views of the Delaware River during the tour. You
should have a great affinity for dogs to do this tour. On
snow tours, you get to stand on the back of the sled and
completely control the huskies. Guests should be nimble,
able to get in and out of a UTV, off and on a sled, and be
able to push the sled when necessary. The maximum

weight for the huskies to pull is 300 lb. Reservations are required.

https://www.arcticpawsdogsledtours.com/

Image by Viola ' from Pixabay

23. Air Tours: Moyer Aviation

Moyer Aviation

Pocono Mountains Airport 188 Airport Drive, Toby-hanna 18466 (570)839-7161

Moyer aviation offers the following air tours: Mountain Tour (centers on Mt. Pocono and shows off the region's many lakes, mountains, and resorts), Delaware Water Gap Tour (heads south and takes you past Pocono Manor, Big Pocono State Park, Stroudsburg, and the gorgeous Delaware Water Gap), Lake Harmony (Highlights many of the lakes that sprinkle the top of the mountain; also seen are Pocono Raceway, Lake Harmony, and the ski slopes of that area), Lake Wallenpaupack Tour (Flies by Tobyhanna Army

Depot, multiple State Parks, and Lake Wallenpaupack itself. It ends by passes Skytop and Buck Hill Falls), Combination Tour (Fly by the Delaware Water Gap and Lake Wallenpaupack in one panoramic tour; or see Lake Harmony and Lake Wallenpaupack together), Customized Tour (Would you like to see sunrise or sunset from the air? Maybe you have a particular location you'd like to visit? Birthdays, anniversaries, and other special occasions can be arranged by special request). Or ask the ultimate question..." Will you spend the rest of your life with me?" in the skies above the Poconos. What better place to start your lives together than high above one of the most romantic areas in the country?

I'm lucky because my Uncle Rob has his own plane to take us on air tours of the Poconos, which he has dubbed Rob Air. But when I asked him who was the second-best for air tours, he said Moyer Aviation. High praise indeed.

http://moyeraviation.com/

My Uncle Rob and I flying over the Poconos in his plane.

24. Cherry Valley Vineyard aka Sorrenti Family Estate

130 Lower Cherry Valley Road Saylorsburg 18353 (570) 992 - 2255

Immigrant Francesantonio Sorrenti founded Sorrenti Winery in 1981. Their original wine is made from fruit and the local Vitis Lambrusca grapes. Sorrenti set the standard for winemakers and wineries in the region. The winery offers Guided Wine Tastings, DIY Tasting Flights, and Spirit Tasting Flights. On the premises is Mama Lucia's Brick Oven Pizzeria. Their unique pizza oven fires pizzas at 750 degrees, making pizzas crusty on the outside and soft on the inside. Their flour is imported from Italy, and their sauces are infused with their wines-yum! On Fridays, Saturdays, and Sundays, various live music acts perform. Other winery events include wine, goat yoga, and paint and sips. Children and pets are allowed (outside only for the pets), and large groups are accommodated. The winery is located on Cherry Valley National Wildlife Refuge (the Sorrenti family donated the land). The trailhead and entrance to the park are 150 meters from the winery parking lot. Other attractions in the area are a big flea market, a corn maze in the fall (I have been it is so much fun and easy to get lost in), and a haunted house.

https://www.sorrentifamilyestate.com/

Image by Jill Wellington from Pixabay

25. Klues Escape Room

542 Main St, Stroudsburg 18360 (570) 688-6950

In the mood for solving puzzles and working as a team with family and friends? Then Klues Escape Room is the place for you. Located in the heart of picturesque downtown Stroudsburg, Klues Escape Room offers four different escape rooms: The Mad Hatter, The Curse of the Pharaoh, The Mad Scientist, and The Moonshiner. They all sound so interesting; I would have trouble choosing!

https://klues.com/

26. Schisler Museum of Wildlife & Natural History and McMunn Planetarium

200 East Prospect Street, East Stroudsburg 18301 (570)422-2705

Located in the Hoeffner Science and Technology Center on the Campus of East Stroudsburg University, this unique science center offers guests the chance to appreciate the wonders of nature and astronomy all in one location. Both the museum and the planetarium are included in the price of admission. The planetarium offers professionally produced films with dazzling imagery from NASA, educational animations, and groundbreaking scientific content. https://www.esu.edu/museum/index.cfm

Image by CollectingPixels from Pixabay

Chapter Two

Pike County

1. Lackawaxen River Swimming Hole

274 River Road, Beach Lake 18405

The Lackawaxen River is a tributary of the Delaware River popular for swimming. People also kayak down the Lackawaxen. Fly fishing is also especially popular on the river as well.

https://www.onlyinyourstate.com/pennsylvania/pa-swimming-holes/

2. Hackers Falls

105 Fisher Ln, Milford, PA 18337

Hackers trail is a 1.4-mile (one-way) moderate hike in the Delaware Water Gap National Recreation Area. The hike will take you up and down hillsides and through the beautiful forests as you wind your way to Hackers Falls. The waterfall has a broad shape, sliding over a precipitous but small drop. Hackers Trail ends at Buchanan Trail, 0.4 mi from Cliff Park trailhead. You can connect trails in the Cliff Park area to create a hike of over 8 miles in the Cliff Park area, filling an entire day. https://www.nps.gov/dewa/planyourvisit/hackers-trail.htm

3. Costa's Family Fun Park

211 Route 6 Hawley 18428 (570)226-8585

Costa's Family Fun Park offers a little bit of fun for every family member. They have go-karts, batting cages, a golf practice range, water slides, mini-golf, laser tag, bumper boats, a children's play place, gem mining, and interactive virtual reality mini-games. There is no fee for general admission, and the activities are either a la carte or bought in a wristband package (which is the most economical if you do more than two activities). The multi-activity summer wristband package includes two go-kart rides, one basket of balls at the driving range, unlimited laser tag, unlimited bumper boats, unlimited mini golf, unlimited water slides, virtual reality mini-games, and entrance to the children's playland. A snack bar offers a variety of children's favorites such as burgers, chicken tenders, and hot dogs. Also offered are salads, snacks, soft-serve, or hand-dipped Hershey's ice cream for dessert.

https://www.costasfamilyfunpark.com/

Image by Lauren E Robins

4. Bushkill Falls

138 Bushkill Falls Trail, Bushkill, PA (570)588-6682

Bushkill Falls comprises approximately 300 acres, eight waterfalls, and greater than 2 miles of hiking trails, bridges, and walkways. Fortunately, it is only a short distance from the primary observation deck if one wishes to see the Main Falls. Three additional hiking trails provide extensive viewing angles of all eight waterfalls. The trails vary in difficulty and length, though there is something for every age and ability. See the website below for chart listing trails and descriptions. Bushkill Falls is privately owned, and tickets must be purchased at the Entrance Building, which also houses the Wildlife exhibit. All trails start behind this building. Backpacks are allowed but picnicking on the trail is discouraged due to the threat of being pursued by wildlife for your food. There is, however, a picnic area if one wishes to picnic.

Snacks are available at the souvenir shop in the snack bar located in the main building. There are several souvenir shops gathered together to resemble a cute village. The Main Stand, Nature Nook, Trading Post (containing Native American mementos), outfitters (hiking apparel), and fudge kitchen. (many flavors of fudge plus Hershey's hand-dipped ice cream, ice cream sodas, and sundaes served in a souvenir mug). You can also mine for gemstones by purchasing a bag of "mining rough" through which you sift through the contents in the sluice (a trough with circulating water) and uncover various gems which are yours to keep. You will receive a card identifying each gemstone found. Fishing is available along the shoreline of Twin Lakes. A PA fishing license is not required, but a permit purchased from them and a current admission ticket are needed.

The PA Wildlife Exhibit, located in the Entrance Building, has a great display of native wildlife. There is a Native American Exhibit featuring a true-to-life longhouse with a smoke hole that would allow cooking and oxygen into the house. There is a display of cooking utensils and hunting equipment to evoke the Native American way of life. Also, at Bushkill Falls is an exhibit detailing the story of the falls. It takes you back into history, when the founder Charles R. Peters opened Bushkill Falls in 1904 with advertising, postcards, souvenirs, and family photographs. Also at Bushkill Falls is the Bushkill Falls Mining Company Maze which challenges you to make your way through a complex maze that will have you competing with family members for the best time.

https://www.visitbushkillfalls.com/

Image from Stockvault

5. Woodloch

731 Welcome Lake Rd, Hawley 18428 (800) WOOD-LOCH Option#1

Woodloch was voted the number one family resort by USA Today and was in the top ten best reader's choice for family resorts also for USA Today in 2021. I haven't included many lodgings in this book because it isn't an activity, but Woodloch is an exceptional place to visit. Unfortunately, most of the activities are for guests of the resort. You can, however, book a day pass at the spa located at The Lodge at Woodloch, which I hear is a fabulous spa. Nonetheless, I will list the activities available to resort guests. First off, there are the Woodloch Resort rooms, all-inclusive plan vacation rental properties, and Woodloch Springs vacation rentals (this housing gives you the option of having a meal plan or not). For the most part, Woodloch is an all-inclusive resort. Your stay offers you a dining plan, activities and amenities, entertainment, and something they call The Woodloch Experience that brings friends and families together to create lifelong memories while having wholesome fun. With over 30 activities scheduled daily, there is something to keep everyone in your family occupied and having fun. Favorites include a petting zoo, bakery wars, athletic contests, and scavenger hunts. The resort amenities include an indoor splash zone, disc golf, scenic boat rides, and go-karts. If you want to try something new, why not take an art class, go on a VR experience, or attempt an escape room? Entertainment includes magicians, live music, and comedians. For children ten and under, there is a Kids Program that offers a variety of activities for your youngsters. Babysitters can watch your children and take them to activities, but spending time with them is encouraged at Woodloch. Also at Woodloch is an Award-Winning Golf Course. The Country Club at Woodloch Springs has been recognized nationally by GOLF Magazine as "One of the finest courses in America." Golf Digest has named Woodloch one of their "Best Places to Play," with a "4.5 Star" rating for the past 26 years. There is also a Performance Studio and Virtual Golf Guide on the premises.

The spa at Woodloch is located in a separate building called The Lodge at Woodloch. They offer a wide variety of massages, facials, body treatments, bodywork, prenatal treatments, couples treatments, treatments for him, and float therapy. Also at the Lodge is the Lotus Salon which does hair and nail services. Tree Restaurant is set in the treetops for dining at the Lodge and serves gourmet fare with locally grown produce. In addition to regular dining at the Tree, there are cooking demonstrations, dinners hosted by the Chef, and seasonal events. If you prefer, you can also choose to stay at the Lodge at Woodloch for more adult accommodations. If you select the complete spa package, your package includes accommodations, three consecutive gourmet meals per night of stay, full use of the spa and fitness center, access to a wide variety of daily class offerings, cooking and baking demonstrations, outdoor activities, and special presentations, You also get a built-in spa credit of $150 per person, per night of stay.

https://www.woodloch.com/
https://www.thelodgeatwoodloch.com/

6. Gray Towers National Historic Site ✦ Borough of Milford

122 Old Owego Turnpike, Milford 18337 (570)296-9630

Gray Towers is considered the birthplace of the American conservation movement. It is worth visiting Gray Towers to see the magnificent mansion, built by local craftsmen and representing the gilded era at its most extravagant. Gray Towers was originally the summer estate of the James Pinchot family and later the main estate of Gifford

Pinchot, who founded the USDA Forest Service. Gifford is known as the father of the conservation movement in the US. Visitors can take guided tours of the mansion and grounds. The grounds are open from sunrise to sunset year-round. Highlights include The Bait Box, which was built in 1926 as a playhouse for the Pinchot's son Gifford Jr, The Letterbox, a small cottage where Gifford Sr corresponded with politicians, artists, and intellectuals of the day, and a fantastic table called The Fingerbowl, an oval-shaped table with the center being filled with water. Food was passed by floating it in wooden bowls across the table. There are also short hiking trails and conservation programs for visitors of all ages. Close by is the Laurel Hill Cemetery, the borough of Milford's first cemetery, with the oldest grave dating back to 1810. The Pinchots built or used 15 sites in the borough of Milford, and you can see them all on the "Pinchot's and Milford Self-Guided Walking Tour ". Check out the borough of Milford while you're there. It has so much to offer. There is plenty to see and do in Milford, from festivals to antiquing to one of America's oldest roads.

https://greytowers.org/
https://milfordpa.us/

Image by smartmdblond from Pixabay

7. The Pike County Historical Society and The Columns Museum

608 BROAD STREET, Milford 18337 (570)296-8126

The Columns Museum has 100's of artifacts, but to me, you visit to see the Lincoln Flag, which is the American Flag that cradled the President's head as he lay dying in Ford's Theater. What a piece of history! The artifacts and historical exhibits in the museum are housed in a two-story, 22-room mansion built in 1904 in the Neoclassical style. It is a gorgeous mansion worth visiting alone, even without the artifacts-the stained glass alone is stunning! The museum also contains an original, wholly restored, roadworthy Abbott and Downing Concord Stage Coach, which can be rented for special events.

http://pikehistorical.org/

Image by Lauren Robins

8. Upper Delaware Scenic and Recreational River- Fishing

This unique area is full of beauty and biodiversity, making it well worth visiting for nature lovers. The unsullied waters of the Delaware River are home to multiple species of fish, thus creating perfect conditions for the angler. A valid New York or Pennsylvania fishing license is required for all those fishing, age 16 and older, on the Delaware River between NY and PA when fishing from a boat or either shore. New Jersey licenses are not valid on the river between New York and Pennsylvania.

Be sure to obtain a summary book of laws and regulations with your license. Refer to the boundary/border waters section and follow the size, creel limit, and open season rules. An angler may use a maximum of two lines. Trout stamps are required with a PA license to take, kill, or possess any trout.

Fishing licenses may be purchased from local sporting goods stores or other state license issuing agents.

Keep an eye out for Fish-For-Free Days during National Fishing Week in June. Along the Upper Delaware, a license is not required on these days; all other regulations still apply, however.

State registration is required for all motorized vessels using the river.

Life Jackets are required for all boaters on the Delaware River. Children 12 years old and younger must wear their life jackets at all times while boating on the river. Please be sure you are practicing responsible angling for the sake of mother nature: 1) keep only the fish you plan to use 2) handle fish gently to avoid injury (if fish don't swim when put back into the water, you can gently glide them back and forth to get oxygen into their gills which should perk them back up) 3) follow all fishing regulations 4) observe safe angling and boating 5) never, ever stock fish or plants in public waters-this is how we get invasive species which are impossible to eradicate 6) do not disturb nesting birds 7) remove all mud and drain all water from boats before departing access site 8) do not release live bait into water 9) dispose of water from bait bucket on land 10) do not transport fish or aquatic plants from one body of water to another 11) do not dispose of fish carcasses or by-products in the water 12) leave no trace

See the website below for maps of fishing areas.

https://www.nps.gov/upde/planyourvisit/fishing.htm
https://www.nps.gov/upde/planyourvisit/maps.htm

Image by Laura Stanley

9. The Upper Mill

150 Water Street, Milford 18337 (570)296-2383

Through the windows of the Waterwheel Cafe Bakery & Bar, you can view a working 24 ft waterwheel and grist mill built in the 1800s. It was one of six first mills that supplied the borough of Milford with cornmeal, animal feed, and various flours. A self-guided tour educates you on turning grain into multiple products using the power of falling water. The Waterwheel Cafe Bakery and Bar is popular for breakfast, lunch, brunch, and dinner when the Chef prepares contemporary cuisine with flavors from Vietnam. We visited recently and had a delicious meal followed by an interesting tour of the grist mill. What surprised me the most was that our 7-year-old daughter loved the tour so much that she said she wanted to come back and eat there again!

https://www.waterwheelcafe.com/upper-mill-grist-mill-milford-pa-pike-county-pa-restaurant/

https://www.waterwheelcafe.com/

Image by Lauren E. Robins

10. Golfing at Paupack Hills

125 Country Club Rd, Greentown 18426 (570)857-0251

The golf course at Paupack Hills is a regulation 18-hole course designed by Tom Fazio. Nestled amongst the trees and offering spectacular views, the course is on its way to being the top-rated course in Pennsylvania. The nice part about golfing at Paupack Hills is that you never feel rushed by other golfers as you traverse the course. Paupack Hills has multiple gorgeous vacation homes for rent, with many housing up to 16 people if you need lodging in the area. They also have a restaurant 13 minutes away by car, The Boat House, on the waterfront of Lake Wallenpaupack, which has become a popular spot on the lake due to its natural beauty and ability to view the stunning sunsets while you dine.

http://paupackhills.com/

Image by Angus Fraser from Pixabay

11. Zane Gray Museum

135 SCENIC DR, Lackawaxen 18435 (570)685-4871

Zane Gray (born in Ohio in 1872) started as a baseball player and became so good that he was offered a scholarship to the University of Pennsylvania's Dental Department. After graduation, he moved to New York to establish his dental practice but continued to play baseball. As a respite from city life, he would visit Lackawaxen, Pennsylvania, where he would fish and enjoy nature. Gray met his wife in 1900, who encouraged him to continue attempting to publish his writings despite recent rejections, for writing was truly a dream of Gray's. By 1905 he had published an article and a novel and had left dentistry to focus full-time on his writing career. The couple settled in a farmhouse overlooking the confluence of the Lackawaxen and Delaware Rivers. Gray became a successful writer, tried his hand in the burgeoning motion picture industry, forming Zane Gray Productions, and during the height of the Great Depression, was able to travel the world pursuing his favorite sport of fishing. The Zane Gray Museum is located in the house once occupied by the Grays and is full of memorabilia, photographs, books, artwork, etc. The museum offers a self-guided tour with National Park Service Rangers available to answer any questions you may have. On sale are a variety of Zane Gray books currently in print. Only in this museum can you get a hint of the diverse life of one of the USA's most popular and widely read western writers.

https://www.nps.gov/upde/learn/historyculture/zanegrey.htm

Image by Angus Fraser from Pixabay

12. Pocono Environmental Education Center

538 Emery Rd, Dingmans Ferry 18328 (570)828-2319

PEEC's mission is to promote environmental awareness, sustainable living, and appreciation of nature through hands-on experience in a National Park. The gorgeous yet sustainably designed building is full of floor-to-ceiling windows letting in natural light and views of nature that has won approximately eight design awards. PEEC is situated within the 77,000 acres of the Delaware Water Gap National Recreation Area and is home to 14 miles of hiking trails open to the public. PEEC offers school programs, meetings and retreats, public programs and workshops, summer camps, and scout programs. It also offers Family Camp Weekends on specific dates throughout the year. Included are lodging, meals, and activities. You can opt to stay in a private PEEC cabin (with heat, electricity, and a private bath) or a yurt (with heat, electricity, and an adjacent bathhouse). Activities could include canoeing, live animal presentations, campfires, guided hikes, etc. Public programs and workshops offer seasonal, family-oriented activities such as canoeing, crafts, cross-country skiing, hiking, orienteering, natural history, field trips to areas of local interest, and more. These programs and workshops are open to educators, families, naturalists, and the general public. PEEC is working towards a more sustainable world filled with tomorrow's environmentally responsible leaders. I think that's something we all can get behind.

https://www.peec.org/

Image by PublicDomainImages from Pixabay

13. Hiking

Lower Hornbecks Creek Trail

Located at mile marker 10.4 on US 209 (just south of Chestnut Hill Road), a short gravel drive to the trailhead.

This hike is an easy 1-mile (one-way) journey ending in a beautiful waterfall. This hike is considered one of the secret gems of the Delaware Water Gap National Recreation Area. Also known to locals as Indian Ladders, the trail follows an old roadbed that winds along Hornbecks Creek. A second waterfall may be accessed from the Upper Hornbecks Creek Trail at the Pocono Environmental Education Center. A reminder that no swimming is allowed within 50 ft upstream of any waterfall or in the waterfalls themselves.

https://www.nps.gov/dewa/planyourvisit/hornbecks-creek-trail.htm

14. Eagle Watching

176 Scenic Drive Lackawaxen 18435 (570)226-3164

The Delaware Highlands Conservancy offers guided tours of eagle habitats and provides maps for those who want to go eagle-watching solo. They have volunteers to answer questions and help visitors spot eagles at common viewing sites. Guests are encouraged to stop first at the winter field office in Lackawaxen to watch an educational video, obtain information, and get educated about the best eagle sightings before heading out to spot some eagles. This inexpensive winter activity is fun for the entire family, especially kids. A tip for spotting eagles is that they are most easily seen from sunrise to a little before noon. Binoculars are best for viewing as the eagles are disturbed by people attempting to get closer on foot.

http://explorepahistory.com/attraction.php?id=1-B-2C35

https://delawarehighlands.org/wp-content/uploads/eagle_observation_blind-map.pdf

Image by ASSY from Pixabay

15. Indian Head Canoes and Rafts

1138 Delaware Drive, Matamoras 18336 (845)557-8777

River trips range from a couple of hours to full-day excursions. Trips in Matamoras can be either rafting, canoeing, or kayaking. This section of the Delaware River is considered the best area for whitewater, and the river itself is a class II river. Because of this, little or no experience is required to have fun. This is a beginner's river, and it is ideal for children. They must be at least 30 lb to ride in rafts and 50 lb in canoe/kayaks. Children ages 12 and under must wear their life preserver at all times. For any trip, remember to pack your swimsuit, lunch, and camera so you can capture all the memories being made on the beautiful Delaware River. River trips go out rain or shine. If the company declares it a rain day, guests will receive a raincheck for that day's river activity with one or more hours' notice before check-in time. These are good for one year from the day of issue. Trips canceled with less than 1 hour's notice before check-in or for groups that do not show up, regardless of weather, will forfeit their deposit and not receive a raincheck.

- Class I River Rapids – Easy, small regular waves, minimal steering necessary.
- Class II River Rapids – Slightly more difficult with small drops and waves.
- Class III River Rapids – Numerous, irregular waves with drops and holes.
- Class IV River Rapids – Very difficult with cross-currents, fast water, and large irregular waves.

- Class V River Rapids – Extremely difficult with exploding waves, fast and powerful currents, cross-currents, large drops, and heavily obstructed riverbeds. Requires skill to navigate.
- Class VI River Rapids – Ultimate limit of navigability.

https://www.indianheadcanoes.com/

Image by Seamus Robins

16. Ski Big Bear at Masthope Mountain

192 Karl Hope Blvd, Lackawaxen 18435 (570)226-8585

Ski Big Bear offers 18 trails, seven lifts, including 3 Magic Carpet lifts, and 650′ of vertical. And bonus, when Mother Nature isn't sending snow, their snowmakers ensure the trails are blanketed with as much snow as possible. Their trails offer something for every ability, which makes

Ski Big Bear a great place to learn or grow in the sport. Lessons are available for skiing and snowboarding, including "learn to" packages. Also offered at Big Bear is snow tubing, perfect for those intimidated by skiing or snowboarding. No special equipment or lessons are needed, just bring yourself, friends, and family and be ready for fun. Their snow tubing hill is sure to thrill and excite you. The mountain has a magic carpet lift for their tubing, so it is unnecessary to trek back up the hill for another ride. Advance online ticket purchases are strongly recommended. Don't arrive late, or you will forfeit the time missed. All tubers must be at least 42" tall, even if tubing with an adult. Double tubes allow the child to ride next to an adult/parent, but children may not ride on laps.

https://www.ski-bigbear.com/

Picture by Kostiantyn Li

17. The Artery- Fine Art and Craft Gallery

210 BROAD STREET, Milford 18337 (570)409-1234

If you're an art lover visiting beautiful, historic Milford, stop at the Artery. The Artery is an artist cooperative located in downtown Milford's historic Forest Hall building. Their gallery hosts a diverse collection of successful and up-and-coming artists from the Tri-State area, whose work has been shown in galleries throughout the United States and Europe, in cities such as New York, San Francisco, Santa Fe, Albuquerque, Philadelphia, Providence, and Paris. The gallery has a wide assortment of artwork available for purchase, such as oil acrylics, watercolor paintings, photography, sculpture, ceramics, and jewelry. The Artery exhibits 10-15 artists at a time, rotating every month. Every second Saturday of the month, they hold a reception to present their featured artist. This coincides with Milford's "Art After Dark" event. Since the Artery is a cooperative, you can meet and speak to artists about any art you'd like to purchase.

https://www.arterygallerymilford.com/

18. Raymondskill Falls

917 Raymondskill Rd, Milford 18337

Delaware Water Gap National Recreation Area (570)426-2452

Even though Bushkill Falls in Monroe County is known as the Niagara Falls of Pennsylvania, Raymondskill Falls is Pennsylvania's largest and tallest waterfall. It is a three-tiered waterfall, and if you add all the drops from each level together, the waterfall is only a few feet shorter than Niagara Falls. It is an easy to moderate 0.3 miles (one way) hike to the falls. Caution is warranted because it is steep and uneven sometimes, although it is a short hike. An upper viewing area provides a view of the upper pool and the top of one of the drops, and a lower viewing area provides spectacular photos of the falls. There is a restroom located at the trailhead. New in 2022 is a hiker shuttle. Visitors should park at North Contact Station/Milford Knob Trailhead parking, and they will be shuttled to Raymondskill Falls. The shuttle parking is located at 165 Rt 209, Milford. To view shuttle routes and schedules, visit the MCTA Hiker Shuttle Website: https://www.gomcta.com/trip.php

Image by Lauren E. Robins

19. Roebling Aqueduct

74 River Road, Beach Lake 18405

Roebling's Aqueduct is the oldest existing wire suspension cable bridge in the US. It was built in 1848 by famous engineer John A. Roebling, who would later design the Brooklyn Bridge. The closing of the Delaware canal led to the end of the use of the aqueduct. It was then converted into a private toll bridge. Around the turn of the century, Charles Spruks built a toll house next to the New York side of the bridge. The aqueduct would function as a means of passage for vehicles until 1979. In 1980, the National Park Service bought the aqueduct to be preserved as part of the Upper Delaware Scenic and Recreational River. What's fascinating to me is that you can walk over the aqueduct today and follow the same path taken by canal travelers and their mules nearly 200 years ago. Self-guided exhibits and historical photographs are located in the Tollhouse on the Minisink Ford, NY side of the bridge. The bridge is also a great place to witness the beauty of the Delaware River and, if you're lucky, several year-round nesting eagles.

https://scenicwilddelawareriver.com/entries/roeblings-delaware-aqueduct-roebling-bridge-upper-delaware-pa-ny/93c62f22-f38d-42f9-b4d5-8ceof83e9f3f

20. Kittatinny

1147 Delaware Drive, Matamoras 18336 (800)356-2852

Kittatinny offers you the opportunity to take multiple adventure trips down the Delaware River: kayaking, rafting, or canoeing. Whichever mode of transportation you choose, you're sure to have fun and enjoy the Delaware River's beauty. All Kittatinny's river trips are unguided, but you will be educated and provided with the tools to have a safe and fun day on the river. Other adventures include paintball and zip lining.

Kayaking

Kittatinny offers open cockpit touring kayaks that are easy to use and will help you navigate some of the most breathtaking stretches of the Delaware River. You can choose a solo kayak or a tandem with a buddy. One-way transportation is included. A life jacket and safety briefing are provided. Children ages four and up are ok to kayak but must weigh at least 40 lb. To solo kayak, you must be 12 years of age or older. If you book 24 hours or more in advance, you can save $5/person from the regular price of the trip. Trip times listed are approximate and vary on river conditions. See the website below for choices of kayak trips.

Rafting

Rafting on the Delaware River is a perfect activity for beginners, those with children, and large groups. The River is crystal clear and full of rapids all season long. Rafting trips take you along cliffs, underneath bridges, and past gorgeous rock formations. Breathe in the fresh air and enjoy the panoramic vistas only viewed by boat. When the river calms down, it's a perfect time for a picnic lunch. One way transportation is included as are life jackets and a safety briefing. Children ages four and up are allowed on rafting trips as long as they weigh at least 40 lb. Rafts can hold a maximum of 6 people, a minimum of 2 people on weekdays, and three on weekends and holidays. You can save $5/person if you book 24 hours or more in advance. Rafting times down the river vary based on conditions.

If you need lodging, Kittatinny has a River Beach campground and cabins. There is also RV parking should you need that. River Beach also offers tubing trips down the river. At the K-Camp location, only 20 miles away in Barryville, NY, you can play a round or two of paintball on their unique mountain top course while dodging and hiding behind boulders and trees. Also at K-Camp is Kittatinny's dual racing zip lines, one of the largest in the US. Drop 36 stories, 150 feet in the air traveling at 40-60 miles per hour as you race the person next to you down Kittatinny's private mountain. You must be eight years or older to ride and between 60-250 lb. Closed-toed shoes are required.

<u>https://kittatinny.com/directions/matamoras-base/</u>

Image by ASSY from Pixabay

21. Shohola Falls

Route 6, Shohola 18458 (570)675-1143

Shohola Falls is known to be one of the least visited, easiest to reach, and a waterfall that puts on a dramatic display of Mother Nature's forces. You can find Shohola falls 10 miles NW of Milford in State Game Lands 180, which is an 11,000-acre protected land comprising mainly the Shohola Marsh Reservoir. Shohola Falls appears to cascade with just as much water no matter how much rainfall there has been, which is unique compared to other falls. Shohola creek takes a 90-degree turn allowing you to view the falls from three sides, another unique feature. The ideal views of the falls are directly in front of them, enabling you to capture them in all their glory. If you wish to visit the opposite side of the falls, you can access it from the parking lot directly off Route 6.

https://www.poconomountains.com/listing/shohola-falls/1680/

https://uncoveringpa.com/how-to-get-to-shohola-falls-in-pike-county-pennsylvania

Image by Gerald Berliner

22. Dingmans & Silverthread Falls

Image by Lauren E. Robins

Dingmans Falls

224 Dingmans Falls Road, Dingmans Ferry 18328 (570)828-2253

Dingmans Creek Trail is the most popular adventure in the Delaware Water Gap National Recreation area. There is a sturdy walking bridge over Dingmans Creek and wooden and Trex™ walkways with rustic benches dotting the path. There are plenty of handholds along most of the walkway, especially where the walkway is slightly elevated. Use caution, however, on any wet walkway surfaces.

Since the Dingmans Creek Trail is one of the most

popular sites within the park, parking fills up quickly, so guests are advised to arrive early in the day to avoid crowds and secure parking. Recommended times to visit this site are either in the spring after a strong rain storm, the first or second week of July when the rhododendrons bloom all along the trail, or for the adventurous hiker, wintertime when the falls are covered in ice and snow shoes or cross-country skis are the preferred way to travel the trail.

Image by Lauren E. Robins

Silverthread Falls

Silverthread Falls is a skinny fall that is nonetheless just as impressive as Dingmans falls. The trailhead for these falls starts at Dingmans Falls Visitor Center, which is off US 209 just south of the 209/739 Junction. From the parking lot, it is a leisurely stroll of 200 feet on a boardwalk to the base of the falls.

Climbing of waterfalls, waterfall pools, or adjacent cliffs is forbidden

There is no swimming or water in water within 50 feet upstream of a waterfall except for individuals engaged in ice climbing

http://gowaterfalling.com/waterfalls/silverthread.shtml

https://www.nps.gov/dewa/planyourvisit/dingmans-creek-trail.htm

Image by Lauren E. Robins

23. Milford Beach

150 MILFORD BEACH RD, Milford 18337

Milford Beach is the perfect place to rest, relax, and cool off after exploring the park at the north end of the Delaware Water Gap National Recreation Area. Milford Beach is a grassy beach offering picnic areas, a pavilion, restrooms, a boat and canoe launch, and access to the Joseph M. McDade Recreational Trail. Milford Beach is sometimes staffed with lifeguards-check the NPS website listed below for information on when. There are no grills present, but you can bring your own. Unfortunately, alcohol and pets are not permitted. Fees are assessed at Milford Beach from April through October. Plenty of activities are nearby if lazing on the beach isn't your style. The George W. Childs Park Trail is only 15 minutes away, and Dingmans Falls is 20 minutes from the beach. Another idea is visiting the Pocono Environmental Education Center, which was discussed in-depth earlier in this book. Also, don't forget that the Delaware National Water Gap Recreation Area has 67,000 acres of nature with 100 miles of hiking trails to explore.

When swimming, be cautious as the currents can be deceptive. Many people have drowned trying to swim across the river. The use of swimming aids, water toys, and floatation devices is prohibited. In general, swimming is not allowed within 50 feet of a boat or canoe launch or the top of any waterfall.

https://www.nps.gov/dewa/planyourvisit/swim.htm

https://www.outdoorproject.com/united-states/penn sylvania/milford-beach

24. Log Tavern Brewing Company

309 E. Harford Street Building-2, Milford 18337

Log Tavern Brewing Company began with a zeal for home brewing and a quest for quality craft beers. They had taken that commitment to serve high-quality craft beers and made it a reality when they opened their physical tavern in Milford. They chose Milford for its nature and vast array of outdoor activities, which fits the company's ethos. In addition to flavorful beers, they serve yummy foods such as personal pizzas, churros, soft pretzels, and mozzarella sticks. They welcome friendly, leashed pets in the outdoor garden and tent area. See the website below for current brews on tap.

https://www.logtavernbrewing.com/

Image by moritz320 from Pixabay

25. The Artisan Exchange- American Fine Art and Gifts

2 1 9 Broad Street, Milford 18337 (570)296-5550

The Artisan Exchange is the Pocono's leading fine art gift gallery. There are over 175 American artists represented in the gallery. You have the unique opportunity to buy pieces of their art from this exchange. Artists vary from Dana Drake's pottery to Doug Walpus's wildlife art of taxidermied butterflies, moths, and dragonflies. Visit the website below to see all the artists and their offerings. Or visit the exchange in person and see what strikes your fancy. We visited recently and bought so many Christmas gifts!

https://www.theartisanexchange.com/

Image by Lauren E. Robins

Chapter Three

C arbon County

1. Eckley's Miners Village

2 Eckley Main Street Weatherly 18255 (570) 636-2071

High on top of a mountain ridge sits an authentic 19th-century coal miner's village where you can visit and experience what life was like for the families that powered America during that era. Eckley consists of 50 major structures and 100 outbuildings open to the public around a mile-long main street. They recommend around 2 ½ hours to see the town and exhibits. Besides the laborer's dwellings, other notable buildings include the doctor's office, company store, sports and social club, and band practice house. Eckley's Catholic Church, miner's double, and Episcopal Church are also open to the public on Fridays, Saturdays, and Sundays in this "patch town," weather permitting, are Eckley's Catholic Church, miner's double, and Episcopal Church. There are guided walking tours through the village, some led by former miners or descendants of miners. These tours last approximately 1 ½ hours. They hold Patchtown Days with art, music, history, food, and vendors yearly. The gift shop is located in what was the rectory for the Church of the Immaculate Conception next door to it. Both buildings were built in 1861. The gift shop is chock-a-block with items to buy to remember your experience in the village. These include books, photos, t-shirts, jewelry, mugs, movies, coal car replicas, etc.

http://eckleyminersvillage.com/

2. Lehigh Gorge Scenic Railway in Jim Thorpe

1 Susquehanna St., Jim Thorpe 18229, (570)325-8425

Take a ride on the rails for a historic train ride in a vintage diesel-powered train, some from as early as 1917, as they take you on a scenic journey following the Lehigh River, over bridges, past Glen Onoko, into the Lehigh Gorge State Park, ending up in Old Penn Haven. Majestic cliffs, mountain vistas, and assorted wildlife are viewable along the forested journey. Your ride is 70 minutes round trip and is narrated by the conductor, who highlights points of interest and identifies wildlife seen (chipmunks, snakes, deer, and sometimes even bears). They keep the information interesting for children of all ages and adults. It is a family-friendly excursion, so no alcohol or smoking is allowed. All trains are wheelchair accessible. Friendly, well-behaved dogs are welcome on the train at no charge. There are several different cars from which to choose, from an open-air car where it is easy to walk around and see the sights to a fully climate-controlled car with a domed ceiling for enhanced viewing of the sights, and many options in between. You can even rent the caboose, which holds groups of up to 6 people and offers excellent views off the back on the first leg of the journey. You can talk to the conductor as he points items of note out on the second leg when you are behind the engine. There is also a "bike train" offered several times a year where you can place your personal or rented bike (from Pocono Bike Rentals) on the train and take the hour journey to White Haven, where you will disembark and ride your bike the 25 miles back to Jim Thorpe. The journey is on a gentle downhill slope, but you will still have to pedal most of the way. Most people finish the ride within 3-4 hours, and if it seems intimidating, don't let it be. I saw people's testimonials online saying they had not ridden bikes recently or were "old and out of shape," and they had no trouble and had a great time. Perhaps the beautiful scenery you pass on your bike, including water-falls, keeps you motivated to finish the ride strong. One tip for those unused to riding was to make sure to get a gel seat, or you may have a sore bottom for a few days.

https://www.lgsry.com/

Image by Lauren E. Robins

3. Covered Bridges

Little Gap Covered Bridge

4300 Little Gap Rd, Palmerton 18071

Little Gap Covered Bridge in Lower Towamensing Township is a wooden covered truss bridge spanning Aquashicola creek. It is an impressive example of early bridge architecture that combines the famous arch-supported "Burr Truss" with elements of the "Howe Truss," thus being the first-time metal was incorporated in the form of tie rods in the bridge's construction. Using this method, fresh-cut timbers could be used and the proper tension maintained by tightening the tension of the rods. This unique construction method marks the transition from wood to metal bridges. It is thought that the builder must be a successor of William Howe, a construction contractor in Massachusetts who patented the Howe truss design in 1840. This would make the bridge 120-150 years old. The consensus is that the bridge was built in 1860. The bridge was rebuilt in 1986 to create a metal grate floor.

The Covered Bridge Inn is within walking distance of the bridge, built in the early 1800s on the stagecoach route serving hearty meals to travelers. Today, they do the same thing serving farm and ocean to table fare in a casual atmosphere. I genuinely think it is so neat to be able to dine in a place where generations before us have eaten. While our lives today differ from theirs, most of us are the same, just travelers seeking adventure passing through town.

https://coveredbridgeinn.net/

https://maps.roadtrippers.com/us/palmerton-pa/food-drink/little-gap-covered-bridge

Harrity Covered Bridge

2950 Pohopoco Dr, Lehighton 18325

Harrity Covered Bridge, also known as Bucks Covered Bridge, was built in 1841 and used to span over Pohopoco Creek. It is located in the middle of picturesque Beltzville State Park. In the late 1960s, plans were being made to create Beltzville Lake and flood Big Creek Valley, which would have destroyed the bridge. Residents fought with the Army Corps of Engineers to save the bridge, and they acquiesced, but not after unsuccessfully trying to float the bridge down the lake! Today the bridge sits near the Beltzville Lake Recreation Area over a slight depression in the land. While not over water anymore, it is still a pleasant place to visit, especially given the setting in the State Park. After seeing the bridge, be sure to explore the State Park- I describe it in more detail as a Carbon County activity later in this book.

https://uncoveringpa.com/visiting-the-covered-bridges-in-carbon-county-pa

4. Oktoberfest at Blue Mountain Resort

1660 Blue Mountain Drive, Palmerton 18071 (610) 826-7700

Celebrate the traditions of Germany at the beautiful Blue Mountain resort's annual Oktoberfest celebration. Hear live German music, enjoy Bavarian-style delicacies, dance the polka, play games, and enjoy drinks in the Biergarten. Prost! Event entry is free but limited to 21 and over guests.

https://www.skibluemt.com/upcoming-events/oktoberfest

Image by Brett Sayles

5. Skiing

Big Boulder and Jack Frost

Big Boulder and Jack Frost mountains are sister mountains roughly 20 minutes apart. Big Boulder was founded first by two pioneers in the coal mining industry. Around 1942, the Split Rock Club was built on picturesque Lake Harmony as a company retreat. The club encompassed Split Rock Lodge and the neighboring Hazzard ski slope. The lodge was sold in 1947, and Hazzard ski slope became known as Big Boulder Ski Area. This was the first commercial ski resort in Pennsylvania and where the first snowmaking was employed.

Jack Frost opened in 1972, basing its designs on the successful Big Boulder.

Jack Frost and Big Boulder pride themselves on being

the first ski resort open every year. Lift tickets bought at one location can be used at the other.

Big Boulder

357 Big Boulder Dr, Lake Harmony 18624 (570)443-8425
Big Boulder boasts 15 trails, ten lifts (2 triples, five doubles, one carpet, and two carpet tubing lifts), a summit elevation of 2175', a base elevation of 1700', and a vertical drop of 475'.

Jack Frost

434 Jack Frost Mountain Rd, White Haven 18661 (570)443-8425
Jack Frost has terrain for every skier's ability. They boast 20 trails (4 easier, six more difficult, eight most challenging, and two terrain parks). Lifts include one quad, two triples, six doubles, one carpet, and two surface tubing lifts. They have a summit elevation of 2000', a base elevation of 1400', and a vertical drop of 600'.

Snow tubing is available at both mountains*

What impresses me about these twin resorts and their parent company, Vail Resorts, is their commitment to sustainability and reducing their carbon footprint. They have set a goal of Zero Net Emissions by 2030, Zero Waste to Landfills by 2030, and Zero Operating Impact on Forests and Habitats. The Jack Frost/Big Boulder website explains their outline on how they plan to achieve this.

https://www.jfbb.com/

Blue Mountain Resort

1660 Blue Mountain Drive, Palmerton 18071
(610)826-7700

Blue Mountain features the highest vertical, some of the longest runs, and the most varied terrain in the region. They also have the largest snowmaking systems on the East Coast, which is beneficial because the snowfalls can be spotty in this region. The resort has 40 trails with 14 beginner, six intermediate, 11 expert, and four expert only. It also boasts five terrain parks so that you can work on your tricks and skills. There are 16 lifts to haul skiers up the slopes, so wait times should be minimal. They offer night skiing and snow tubing as well. (See website for summer activities offered.)

https://www.skibluemt.com/

Image by Martin Bisplinghoff from Pixabay

6. Mauch Chunk Lake Park

625 Lentz Trail, Jim Thorpe 18229 (570)325-3669

The Mauch Chunk Lake Park is located in the Boroughs of Jim Thorpe and Summit Hill. The park began as a flood control project because of the mountainous terrain and confinement of the Mauch Chunk Creek that flows beneath the town of Jim Thorpe. Major flooding frequently occurred in the past, and Tropical Storm Agnes blew through just after completion. Had the dam not been completed, it is estimated that $2 million in damages would have occurred. Today the park exceeds 150,000 visitors annually and has become a popular vacation destination for many families for camping, swimming, picnicking, hiking, biking, fishing, and boating.

Camping

The Mauch Chunk Lake Park camping area has modern restroom and shower facilities with hot running water. The camping area offers 135 sites, including lakefront tents, camping cottages, and organized group camping for scout troops and other non-profit organizations. Pavilions with kitchen areas are also available to rent. A Camp Store is conveniently located on the campgrounds that sells firewood, camping supplies, snacks, and novelty items.

BOATING

The Mauch Chunk Lake is 345 acres and has two boat launch areas open year-round for fishing and recreational boating. The Mauch Chunk Lake is only designated for non-powered watercraft and electric motor use. All watercraft must be registered in accordance with PA Fish & Boat Commission rules and regulations. PA Fish & Boat Commission launch permits are available at the park office for non-powered watercraft that do not have a registration. Boat rental is located at Boat Launch A. The boat rental offers canoes, kayaks, rowboats, and paddle boats. Reservations are recommended. The boat rental can be reached at (570) 325-4389 during the operating season.

FISHING

The Mauch Chunk Lake is 345 acres and provides year-round fishing for large-mouth bass, small-mouth bass, walleye, crappie, bluegill, perch, chain pickerel, and catfish. Fishing is permitted anywhere along the shoreline, except a 100' buffer zone around all sides of the swimming area. Fishing is also not allowed from the dam. The fully accessible fishing pier at Boat Launch A is a popular spot during summer. Restroom facilities are available at both boat launches. The boat rental sells live bait such as minnows, leeches, and nightcrawlers. The Mauch Chunk Lake is designated a big bass lake by the PA Fish & Boat Commission, meaning that bass must be at least 15 inches long to take legally. Additional size and creel limits can be found by visiting www.fish.state.pa.us. The Mauch Chunk Creek, located along the Switchback Trail below the lake, provides rainbow and brook trout fishing opportunities. The creek is stocked annually in the spring for the opening day of trout season. Anyone 16 years of age and older must have a Pennsylvania Fishing License. A trout stamp is required (this is in addition to your license and lets you fish specifically for trout). All PA Fish & Boat Commission rules and regulations apply when fishing at the Mauch Chunk Lake Park.

The Mauch Chunk Lake Park is an official site of the Fishing Tackle Loaner Program. Fishing tackle is available to campers free of charge.

BEACH SWIMMING AREA

Beach and swimming area are open Memorial Day weekend through Labor Day. Swimming is permitted only while lifeguards are on duty. The beach area includes play equipment for children, a food and refreshment stand, and a beach pavilion. Summer beach tags can be purchased at the main park office.

Alcoholic beverages are strictly prohibited. Pets are also not permitted.

They do not allow EZ-Up setups on the beach or in the beach area.

PICNICKING

There is a picnic area that is a lakeside wooded picnic grove and is conveniently located within a short walking distance to the beach area. There are plenty of picnic tables and hibachis to choose from. The picnic area offers an excellent view of Mauch Chunk Lake. Covered picnic pavilions can be rented for daily use. Reservations are required in advance. Pavilions can be rented with and without a small kitchen area. Admission to the park is included with pavilion rentals.

HIKING

Plan your next hiking or biking adventure. Mauch Chunk Lake Park offers easy access to the Switchback Railroad Trail (the most popular), leading into downtown Jim Thorpe. Hikers enjoy the scenic Shoreline Trail, while the Fireline Trail offers a fun challenge. The Orchard Trail and Board Bottom Trail are peaceful paths below the dam.

WILDLIFE

The Mauch Chunk Lake Park is 3400 acres of deciduous woodland forest, wetland, open fields, and Eastern White Pine and Hemlock stands. This diverse habitat makes the park excellent for bird watching and wildlife viewing. Examples of wildlife seen are white-tailed deer, gray squirrel, bald eagle, black bears, red foxes, ruffed grouse, cattle egret, wild turkey, wood ducks, common yellowthroat, Great Blue Heron, American woodcock, killdeer, and green heron.

Carbon County Environmental Education Center

The CEEC is located on 60 acres of the beautiful Mauch Chunk Lake Park. It is 2 miles west of the main park entrance. It features nature trails, a waterfowl observatory, butterfly gardens, bird feeding stations, and a boardwalk trail where visitors can view birds of prey: Great-Horned Owls, Red-Tailed Hawks, Golden Eagle, and American Bald Eagle. The facilities are free and are open daily from dawn until dusk. To learn more about the Environmental Center and its programs, visit their website at www.carboneec.org

The Mauch Chunk Lake Park has a strict No Alcohol and No Pets policy. Guests who violate this policy will be issued a citation and are subject to eviction.

https://www.carboncounty.com/index.php/park

Image by Seamus Robins

7. Penn's Peak

325 Maury Rd, Jim Thorpe 18229 (866)605-PEAK

Penn's Peak is a concert venue on a mountaintop in Jim Thorpe overlooking Beltzville Lake and featuring original musical acts, tribute musicians, and more at evening and matinee performances. Penn's Peak also hosts deck parties with various musical acts and scenic views of the lake and mountains. When you are inside the venue, you'll find an area that can seat 1,800, a roomy dance floor, vaulted ceilings, and a restaurant and bar. The venue boasts that you will enjoy excellent views of the acts and ideal acoustics no matter where your seat is located. Also, both have easy access to the bar no matter which level you are located. If you're in Pike county for the evening, check out the events schedule online at the website listed below and enjoy the show!

https://www.pennspeak.com/

Image by Lauren E. Robins

8. Beltzville State Park-Boating, Swimming, Volleyball, Soccer, Hiking, Waterfall

2950 Pohopoco Drive, Lehighton 18235-890 (610)377-0045

This 3,002-acre park offers multiple recreational activities, indeed something for everyone. The park makes for excellent fishing, boating, and birdwatching. The Pohopoco Creek, a perfect trout stream, feeds Beltzville Lake, making it an ideal location for fish and migrating waterfowl. The State Park offers various environmental education and recreation programs from March through October. They include guided walks, hands-on activities, and specialized programs.

The park offers ten hiking trails of varying difficulty and type, totaling 22.9 miles in length.

Picnic areas in the park are located in the Pine Run West Day Use Area. There are also playfields around the wooded picnic areas with an ADA-accessible children's playground between Picnic Pavillion Four and the beach. The park also has four picnic pavilions which may be reserved up to 11 months in advance. Any unreserved pavilions are first come, first serve. Picnic Pavilions #1, 2, and 4 are ADA accessible.

The beach is 525 feet and is open from late May to mid-September, eight am-sunset. Smoking is prohibited entirely on the beach, including uses like e-cigarettes.

Water skiing is allowed in the zoned skiing area along the lake's south shore from sunrise to sunset. All skiing should take place in a counterclockwise direction. Boats not engaged in skiing must remain outside the ski area while skiing is in progress. No more than one water-ski device may be towed on weekends and holidays from the Saturday before Memorial Day through Labor Day. No kite-sailing or parasailing is allowed. Boats may not exceed 45 mph.

Kayaks, paddle boats, and pontoon boats (need advance reservation) can be rented from boat rental concessions west of the swimming beach.

Mountain biking is only allowed on the Christman Trail, 2.5 miles long.

https://www.dcnr.pa.gov/StateParks/FindAPark/
BeltzvilleStatePark/Pages/default.asp

Image by Joe Zlomek on Unsplash

9. Lehigh Gorge State Park

S Lehigh Gorge Dr, Weatherly 18255 (570)443-0400

What makes Lehigh Gorge State Park unique is the geological features present in the park. The gorge is cavernous, precipitous, and surrounded by dense flora, rock protuberances, and beautiful waterfalls.

There are numerous activities to do at the park. The park's website (seen below) lists the top ten activities to do at the park.

Top 10 Activities at Lehigh Gorge

1. Take a group of friends for a bicycle ride (or a hike) along the river on the Lehigh Gorge Trail.
2. Challenge yourself to a whitewater rafting trip.

3. Experience the wonder of the Upper Grand Section of the Lehigh Canal by standing inside Lock 22 at Mud Run.
4. Enjoy the view from the top of Inclined Planes at Penn Haven.
5. Snowmobile the 15-mile trail from Penn Haven to White Haven.
6. Eat a picnic lunch to the beautiful sounds and sights of Buttermilk Falls.
7. Explore Audubon's Lehigh Autotour.
8. Photograph beautiful rhododendrons along the Lehigh Gorge Trail in July.
9. Find your own secret fishing hole in the nearly 30 miles of river or its numerous tributaries.
10. Visit a neighbor- Hickory Run State Park (I will write about that park next)

There are three hiking trails of varying difficulty totaling 35.3 miles.

The areas along rivers are ideal traveling routes for animals and have an impressive display of native flora. Common birds include warblers, Louisiana water thrush, bald eagles, osprey, kingfisher, mergansers, and wild turkeys. Mammals can be found by water, roadways, and trails, including white-tailed deer, black bear, gray and red foxes, beaver, mink, muskrat, and Allegheny wood rat. In the summer, reptiles like fence lizards can be seen along the Lehigh Gorge Trail. Be on the lookout for Northern Copperheads and Timber Rattlesnakes, as well as many other species of snake, and make sure to respect them and give them a wide berth on trails. Beautiful native plant species can be found throughout the park, such as rhododendron, eastern hemlock, black, gray, yellow, and river birch trees, red columbine, purple flowering raspberry, jack in the pulpit, huckleberry, blueberry, witch hazel, and cardinal flowers.

https://www.dcnr.pa.gov/StateParks/FindAPark/ LehighGorgeStatePark/Pages/default.aspx

Wintertime at Lehigh Gorge State Park Image from Stockvault

10. Hickory Run State Park

3613 PA-534, White Haven 18661 (570)442-0400

The website for Hickory Run State Park (see below) lists the

Top 10 Activities to do at the Park:

1. Walk Across Boulder Field.
2. Witness and photograph the magnificent Hawk Falls.
3. Experience the solitude of Stametz Dam along the Shades of Death Trail.

4. Throw a picnic! Play 18 holes of disc golf followed by a picnic in Sand Spring Day Area,
5. View the Lehigh Gorge along the Fireline Trail.
6. Catch a wild brook trout from Hickory Run or Mud Run.
7. Enjoy an ice cream after swimming in Sand Spring Lake.
8. Interact with the exhibits at the visitor center and attend an educational program.
9. Spend the weekend with the family in a rustic camping cottage.
10. Visit a neighbor-Lehigh Gorge State Park.

The park boasts 44 miles of trails that lead you through beautiful and historic areas, particularly when the rhododendron and mountain laurel bloom from mid-June to Mid-July and then again in mid-October when the fall foliage is at its peak of beauty. What's fascinating is that many trails were roads used between 1830 and 1900, so when you are hiking, keep the many generations that have passed on in your mind and wonder what they were thinking, feeling, and doing.

The park hosts over 150 species of birds, 50 species of mammals (such as white-tailed deer, black bears, and minks), and various invertebrates (such as black snakes and timber rattlesnakes). In springtime, look for wood frogs and spotted Jefferson salamanders that migrate to the bogs to breed. In the unglaciated portion of the park, where chestnut oak and beech trees dominate, American redstarts, red-eyed vireos, and scarlet tanagers are commonly found. In contrast, in the campground, which straddles the two areas, you should look and listen for six species of thrush:

American robin, wood thrush, hermit thrush, Swainson's thrush, veery, and Eastern bluebirds.

Other activities in the park include a 19-hold disc golf course in the Sand Spring Day Use Area. It is a flat, moderately wooded course with crushed stone tees and basket holes totaling approximately 1 mile in length. Please be careful of picnickers when playing the first ten holes. You must bring your own recreational equipment as discs are not supplied.

Geocaching, a high-tech treasure hunting game played using GPS, can also be played in the park. Information on hidden geocaches within the park can be found on the website: https://www.geocaching.com/play

In the winter, cross-country skiing can be done on the 14 miles of trails in the park. The trails are not groomed, and you must supply your own skiing equipment.

https://www.dcnr.pa.gov/StateParks/FindAPark/HickoryRunStatePark/Pages/default.aspx

Shades of Death Waterfall Image from Stockvault

11. Adventure Center at Whitewater Challengers

288 N Stagecoach Rd, Weatherly, PA 18255 (800)443-8554

Whitewater Challengers offer three different rafting adventures. Their most popular trip is only available on dam release weekends, several of which are throughout the summer. When the dam releases water, it creates thrilling class 2-3+ rapids. This adventure is only available to those eight years and older. The trip lasts approximately 3-4 hours, depending on weather and water conditions. The next rafting trip is a more leisurely trip down the rapids suitable for the entire family as long as the children are over the age of 4. The trip lasts 2 ½- 3 hours, depending. The final rafting trip is only for those looking for extreme adventure. Billed as the "ultimate challenge," it is called the Rafting Marathon, and it covers approximately 25 miles of river, dozens of rapids, and lasts 5-7 hours, depending. It is only available for those over 12 years of age.

River rapids are classified from I to VI.

- Class I River Rapids – Easy, small regular waves, minimal steering necessary.
- Class II River Rapids – Slightly more difficult with small drops and waves.
- Class III River Rapids – Numerous, irregular waves with drops and holes.
- Class IV River Rapids – Very difficult with cross-currents, fast water, and large irregular waves.
- Class V River Rapids – Extremely difficult with exploding waves, fast and powerful currents,

cross-currents, large drops, and heavily obstructed riverbeds. Requires skill to navigate.
- Class VI River Rapids – Ultimate limit of navigability.

The Lehigh River has Class I, II, and III rapids.

WHITEWATER CHALLENGERS also offer inflatable kayaking, or "ducky," trips. You can choose from a tandem (2-person) or solo kayak. An experienced guide will lead you in their kayak. The journey has you navigating class 2-3 rapids and lasts approximately 2-3 hours. Lunch is included on this adventure.

The adventure center also contains a snack bar with hoagies (don't call them subs or heroes if you are from out of town, or you will be outed as a tourist), a variety of hot foods, ice cream, and coffee.

https://whitewaterchallengers.com/locations/lehigh-river-poconos-pa/

12. Asa Packer Mansion Museum

Packer Hill Ave, Jim Thorpe 18229 (570)325-3229

A visit to the Asa Packer Mansion is not just a visit to an opulent mansion built in the 1800s. It's a view into the life of an extraordinary man and his family that inhabited the magnificent home. Asa Packer came from very humble beginnings but chose to risk it all by buying almost all the controlling stock and interests for the unfinished Delaware, Lehigh, Schuylkill, and Susquehanna Railroads. Because of that venture, he became a self-made man and an incredible philanthropist. The founder of Lehigh University, Asa

Packer, gave away $33 million of his fortune to the town of Mauch Chunk (later known as Jim Thorpe) and the Lehigh Valley. His remaining estate was valued at $54.5 million by the time he died. His daughter was also a philanthropist, and because of her, we have the mansion museum, as she willed it to the town as a monument to her late father.

Tours of the mansion are docent-guided and consist of a detailed history of the Packer family. Visitors can view the original contents of the house built in 1861. Tours can last approximately 45 minutes depending on the group size, number of questions asked, and the level of interest shown. Tours of the mansion are very popular and do sell out, so purchasing as soon as you arrive at the Mansion is recommended.

http://www.asapackermansion.com/

Asa Packer on the Left and Harry Packer on the right
Mansions Image by Seamus Robins

13. Old Jail Museum

128 West Broadway, Jim Thorpe 18229 (570)325-5259

The Old Jail resembles a medieval fortress. Standing at two stories high, it contains 72 rooms. The Old Jail is infamous as the site of the hangings of seven coal miners suspected of being a part of the secret society of "Molly Maguires" in the 1800s. The Old Jail contains a mysterious handprint made by one of the seven men that has to be seen to be believed.

If you are interested in the supernatural and mysterious, you have come to the right place. Many visitors have encountered ghosts or phenomena they can't explain on the Jail's 30-minute guided tours. Tours leave every 20-30 minutes. A Ghost Tour is also offered if you want to hear tales of guests' ghostly experiences in the Old Jail. Be aware that no ghost hunting equipment is allowed.

My seven-year-old daughter and I visited the Old Jail. While we were fascinated with the jail's ins and outs and stories, she was terrified of being down in the dark, freezing dungeon where they housed the men in solitary confinement. I ventured into the cells, but she refused! Will your child be braver?

http://www.theoldjailmuseum.com/

Top left: Old Jail building. Top right: Inside main jail with gallows.
Bottom left: Dungeon cell Bottom right: Sign describing Molly Maguire
executions Photo credit by Lauren E Robins

14. Bear Mountain Butterfly Sanctuary

18 Church Rd, Jim Thorpe 18229 (570)325-4848

Bear Mountain Butterfly Sanctuary is a unique destination where you get to experience feeding live butterflies in an indoor "Flutterarium," learn about exotic frog and fish species, view various creatures such as axolotls and turtles, make crafts with your kids in their art, and activity room, and shop in the nature-based gift shop. In addition to the critters they already housed, in 2021, they added poison dart frogs, Oriental fire belly toads, a white tree frog, red-eared sliders, glow fish, bettas, and two new axolotls. They aspire to add even more to the mix in 2022 and beyond. There is much indoor fun at the Bear Mountain Butterfly Sanctuary, making it a great rainy day activity. Check out the website below for weekly specials and events. Do note that if your child is of toddler age, they recommend that the sanctuary may not be the best place to visit as children can be frightened by butterflies flying at their faces. They recommend a trip to use their outdoor picnic tables when the wild butterflies are feeding on the native pollinator garden planted in front of the Sanctuary in July or August. Wild butterflies are less likely to fly in a child's face. When I visited to take pictures, a toddler came in before me and was not turned away, but they did instruct his mother to keep him in arms the entire time, lest he steps on a butterfly that had landed on the ground. Also of note to parents of youngsters is that strollers are not allowed in the Sanctuary building due to fire code regulations. A child carrier is recommended if possible.

You can purchase butterfly kits at certain times of year to watch them grow from cocoon into a butterfly and then be released. My favorite part about this tradition is the Native American Wish Legend that says: When you take your butterfly outside to release it, whisper a wish to it as you let it go. It will carry your desire to the Great Spirit in the sky because you have set it free and restored the balance of nature.

https://bearmountainbutterflies.com/

Couple feeding butterflies in Flutterarium and various exhibits Image by Lauren E Robins

15. Shopping in Downtown Jim Thorpe

When visiting Jim Thorpe, there is so much to see and do. You can be forgiven if you skip shopping. But I think you are missing out. Not so much on the retail therapy aspect (because, to be sure, I love going into unique stores and, above all, antiquing, both of which you can do here in spades) but because the streets are lined with gorgeous old buildings, many of them painted in beautiful colors. We drove down Race street on our recent visit, and it was as if we had entered Victorian England. Right after, we had passed a 1970s hippie head shop a block or two before that!

There is a wide variety of stores. They even have an old-fashioned 5 & 10 shop that makes me remember the one in my hometown of Winnetka, IL. I will be visiting again and shopping until I've had my fill.

Another adventure we discovered when we stopped in Jim Thorpe to take pictures on the way into town was the Jim Thorpe Trolley. It is a 70-minute trolley ride with historical narration that makes seven stops around the town of Jim Thorpe. You can hop off and on, seeing sites as you please. Had it not been pouring rain and at the end of the day, we would have ridden the trolley—another activity for when we revisit Jim Thorpe.

https://www.jimthorpetrolley.com/

Pretty Building in downtown Jim Thorpe Image by Seamus Robins

16. The Mauch Chunk Opera House

14 W Broadway, Jim Thorpe 18229 (570)325-0249

The historic Mauch Chunk Opera House is one of America's oldest vaudeville theaters still in operation. The building was built in 1881 next to what was known as "Millionaire's Row." It was a whistle-stop for emerging vaudeville stars and a local meeting spot for politicians, merchants, and other dignitaries. The Opera House is constantly being renovated to make positive changes for its guests. It now seats 380 and hosts intimate shows where there isn't a bad seat in the house. Visit the website below to see who plays at the opera house during your trip to Jim Thorpe, aka Mauch Chunk. They host a wide variety of entertainment, ranging from classic rock and jazz to blues, folk, tribute bands, and comedy acts. There is something for everyone, and win-win in an incredibly historical setting.

https://mcohjt.com/

Mauch Chunk Opera House Image by Lauren E. Robins

17. Mauch Chunk Museum and Cultural Center

41 W Broadway, Jim Thorpe 18229 (570)325-9190

The Museum's main exhibition is "The Story of Mauch Chunk." Expert tour guides lead visitors through the museum, discussing the history of Jim Thorpe, from geology that formed the coal in the region during prehistoric times to present-day Jim Thorpe. They discuss how the town was renamed Jim Thorpe, from Mauch Chunk, after famed Olympian Jim Thorpe, who is buried there in a failed attempt to revitalize the town.

Also affiliated with the Museum is the Kemmerer Carriage House and Library, which is a tribute to the millionaires of early Mauch Chunk. It is located at 20 Packer Hill Rd, across from the Asa and Harry Packer Mansions. Your guide will greet you dressed in 1800s attire and regale you with the town's history, which began in 1818.

https://mauchchunkmcc.org/

Mauch Chunk Museum and Cultural Center Image by Lauren E. Robins

18. Pocono Whitewater

1519 State Route 903, Jim Thorpe 18229
(1-800-944-8392)

Pocono Whitewater offers several rafting trips down the Lehigh River ranging from "mild to wild." You can also choose multi-sport packages that combine rafting or inflatable kayaking with biking, hiking, or paintball. You can do these activities during the day or night and over one or two days. PW also offers these activities a la carte.

The Dam Release whitewater rafting in the Lehigh Gorge State Park is a popular adventure for anyone aged eight seeking thrills and fun memories. The trip is 12 miles long and takes approximately 4-5 hours, traveling through 17 sets of Class II-III rapids surrounded by gorgeous mountainous scenery.

The Family Style Whitewater rafting trip is for you if your kiddos are younger. It is a guided, 3-4 hour rafting adventure on the Lehigh, through 8 miles of Class I and II rapids. Ideal for children ages four and older and adults that want to chill more than experience thrills.

Pocono Whitewater also has an exclusive Pirate Whitewater Rafting trip during which the Lehigh River appears to be besieged by invading pirates. Captain Jack and his crew of Pocono Pirates are armed with water cannons and plotting a fierce yet friendly attack on your party's raft. Avast ye mateys hoist up the mainsail! (I couldn't help myself!) You will be traveling through Class I and II rapids during the battle. Included is a free All-You-Can-Eat Riverside Barbecue Lunch. (PS if your family doesn't want to participate in the water battle, they can opt-out, but why would you go on a pirate adventure and not have a water battle?) If you require pirate gear, the "Pirate Cove" area of the souvenir shop has everything you should need.

Another unique trip is the Moonlight Rafting adventures. Exclusive to PW, take a journey down the Lehigh River under the stars and by moonlight. It is an 8-mile guided trip-the guide will help keep you company and on course. Fireflies and glow sticks help light the way. A bonfire, marshmallows, and a glass of wine or two are waiting for you at the journey's end. It creates a unique combination of thrilling romance.

Also on offer from PW is the Expedition, a trip through Lehigh Gorge State Park in an inflatable kayak. While exploring the 12 miles of river, you get an incredible workout and experience the river without other whitewater rafters. River guides will educate you on how to maneuver the kayak, navigate the river swells, and return to your boat in the event of capsizing.

Food is available at the Broken Paddle Bar and Grill. The Broken Paddle is a full-service kitchen with everything you need, breakfast, lunch, or dinner, for a day out on the water.

As an FYI:

River rapids are classified from I to VI.

- Class I River Rapids – Easy, small regular waves, minimal steering necessary.
- Class II River Rapids – Slightly more difficult with small drops and waves.
- Class III River Rapids – Numerous, irregular waves with drops and holes.
- Class IV River Rapids – Very difficult with cross-currents, fast water, and large irregular waves.

- Class V River Rapids – Extremely difficult with exploding waves, fast and powerful currents, cross-currents, large drops, and heavily obstructed riverbeds. Requires skill to navigate.
- Class VI River Rapids – Ultimate limit of navigability.

The Lehigh River has Class I, II, and III rapids.

PW is affiliated with Pocono Biking and offers biking and rafting as part of their adventure packages. In addition to offering bike rentals for five trails totaling 107 miles, Pocono Biking also provides the bikes for the Bike Train (see activity entry on Lehigh Gorge Scenic Railway in Jim Thorpe, Number 9 in Pike county).

https://poconobiking.com/

Paintball at Skirmish is also offered as part of an adventure multisport trip. (See activity entry number 21 in Pike County)

https://www.skirmish.com/

Image from Stockvault

Image by Tom Fisk

19. Jim Thorpe Sidecar Tourz

16 W. Broadway, Jim Thorpe 18229 (570) 249-1570

At Sidecar Tourz, you can take a thrilling ride in a vintage BMW motorcycle sidecar as you travel through scenic and historic Jim Thorpe, aka America's Little Switzerland. They offer several tour packages: The Countryside Scenic Tour (from vista on top of Flagstaff Mountain with a 100-mile view to Blue Mountain countryside and Mauch Chunk Lake Park. Tour can be extended to include

Carbon County and a visit to Carbon County Environmental Center to have a close encounter with a Bald Eagle and a Golden Eagle.), Mountainside Scenic Tour (head through the rhododendrons and mountain laurel up to the summit of Bear Mountain, ending with a visit to Jim Thorpe Memorial Park and the 100-mile view lookout), and Wine Tasting Tour(includes a visit to an award-winning local vineyard with scenic vistas atop Blue Mountain. Also, visit the 100-mile view, Flagstaff Mountain summit, and beautiful Mauch Chunk Lake Park.

- All tours begin and end at the Marion Hose Bar (see address above)
- Helmets with eye protection are provided with all packages. Bring your sunglasses.
- It is advised to wear long pants and sturdy, closed-toe shoes.
- Sidecar Tourz reserves the right to reroute tours as needed.
- Note-they do not rent sidecars, but trips to ride in them.

This would be a great way to check a sidecar ride off your bucket list today!
https://www.jimthorpesidecartourz.com/

20. Broadway Grille *live music on weekends*

24 Broadway, Jim Thorpe 18229 (570)732-4343
Located in the heart of downtown Jim Thorpe, this restaurant associated with the Inn at Jim Thorpe is in a gorgeous Victorian building with pretty ironwork almost

reminiscent of New Orleans-style buildings. They serve breakfast, lunch, dinner, and boxed lunches if you need a meal before your upcoming adventure in Jim Thorpe. The Grille hosts live music that can be heard either in the pub or the Underground, a live music venue underneath the Grille featuring exposed brick walls, a large slate topped bar, tin ceilings, lounge seating, a roomy dance floor, and giant flat-screen TVs. We dined there recently, and my husband had a delicious short rib grilled cheese, I had pulled pork nachos, and our daughter had a burger with fruit (the fruit was blue-berries and strawberries, not your typical melons). I also got a virgin blackberry sour which was delicious, albeit a bit sweet without the bourbon. We ate outside on the upper terrace, and it was lovely. The only downside was the many loud motorcycles that passed, but it was Memorial Day, so this may have enhanced that aspect,

https://broadwaygrillepub.com/

Broadway Grille and Pub Image by Lauren E Robins

21. Skirmish Paintball

211 N Meckesville Rd, Albrightsville, PA 18210
(570) 325-3654

Skirmish is touted as one of the premier paintball arenas in the world. The map covers 750 acres of the Pocono Mountains and contains unique topography that makes paintball here supreme. Such as the dense woods, open fields, bridges, creeks, swamps, forts, villages, rhododendron trees, cargo containers, tanks, TWO castles, airplanes, speedball arenas, and inflatable bunkers. Skirmish truly has everything in a paintball arena. Skirmish provides all the necessary equipment for playing paintball. This includes: paintball referees, paintball gun, goggles, facemask, and N2 air fills. They also have changing rooms, a snack bar, souvenir photos, and a full-service paintball pro-shop for gun and equipment sales. You may bring your own paintball gun if it is not fully automatic. However, you are not allowed to bring your own paintballs. Individuals and groups of all sizes are welcome. We will form paintball teams for individuals or small groups (less than 20 people), let your party stay together, and do our best to match you against a group of equal size and skill. If you have a group of 20 or more, you will play on various private paintball fields all day—just you and your friends!

Note that you must be ten years or older to play paintball.

https://www.skirmish.com/

Image by Christoph Schütz from Pixabay

22. Stabin Museum and Cafe Arielle

268 W Broadway, Jim Thorpe 18229 (570)325-5588

The Stabin Museum is located in a red brick and stone building that features an underground aqueduct exposed rock wall at the base of the mountain that all serves to create an atmosphere as unique as the artist himself.

Victor Stabin was born in Manhattan and began his artistic career at the New York High School of Art and Design. He then attended the Art Center College of Design in Los Angeles and the School of Visual Arts in NYC, where he lived and worked as an illustrator. He left NYC after 25 productive years and moved to Jim Thorpe to create personal work and let his imagination be his only boss. Stabin's artwork defies genre and description. His work is a tribute to the entirety of art history, from centuries-old Japanese watercolors to modern graphic arts. His influences include his family, the connection between man and nature, and water and the water's edge. He is often compared to Dr. Seuss, M.C. Escher, and Salvador Dali as an artist.

The museum is composed of: 1) The Gallery/Sky lounge, where you can view the art during the day, and at night the lights are turned down, and it becomes a lounge for conversations and drinking. 2)The Thing Shop, where you can buy original works of Stabin's such as limited-edition prints, books, and cups. 3)The Screening Room is where you can see some of Stabin's animations and documentaries about his work. 4)The ABC room is where you meet Daedal Doodle, the alliterative dictionary-inspired ABC book that changed everything,

Cafe Arielle is an eatery as unique as Stabin himself. The setting is elevated, but the menu is straightforward yet ever-changing. Ambiance rises to meet flavor. The indoor glass box over the Mauch Chunk Creek has often been compared to Frank Lloyd Wright's Fallingwater. Make sure to visit the Avant-Garden before or after your meal, where you will find an impressive dining patio nestled beneath a rocky outcrop of the mountain's base. The Sunday Jazz Brunch is a can't-miss event if you're in town for it.

http://stabinmuseum.com/

Stabin Museum Image by Seamus Robins

23. No. 9 Coal Mine and Museum

9 Dock St, Lansford 18232 (570)645-7074

Visit a real coal mine and get educated on mining practices in the 18-1900s at the No. 9 Coal Mine and Museum. The No. 9 Coal Mine opened in 1855 and mined a large vein of Anthracite coal, known as the Mammoth Vein, that was the main focus of mining operations for Panther Valley. Early mining operations were not focused on the town of Lansford but rather a town just above it called Summit Hill. The No. 9 Mine operated from 1855 until 1972, making it the longest continuously operated deep Anthracite coal mine globally. After the mine was abandoned, a local group committed to preserving it for future generations and took control of the property in 1992.

Guests to the No. 9 Mine will ride 1,600 feet into the mountain by rail before starting a 600 ft guided walking tour. Visitors can examine the original 700-foot-deep mine shaft, walk the "mule way," and see the miner's hospital, which is carved right into the solid rock of the mine.

Once the mine tour is over, guests visit the museum, located in the original "Wash Shanty," built before the First World War. This museum holds the most extensive collection of mining artifacts in the area. You can see items such as tool blasting equipment, household goods, and much more belonging to the miners who worked in No. 9.

Inside the museum is a gift shop that offers visitors items such as books, carved coal pieces, and t-shirts, among other goods. The site has picnic facilities that are available for large groups.

It is recommended to wear a sweater or light jacket year-round when visiting the mine, as it is 50 degrees down there no matter the weather topside. Please wear closed-toe shoes as the paths in the mine are made of loose gravel.

https://no9minemuseum.wixsite.com/museum

Image by Henryk Niestrój from Pixabay

24. Deer Path Riding Stables

95 PA-940, White Haven 18661 (570)443-4431

Deer Path Riding Stables offers picturesque, guided trail rides lasting an hour in length, including basic instructions before leaving the barn. The trip takes you through various picturesque terrain: forests, open fields, hills, and rhododendron marshes. The latter are carpeted with moss and ferns and fed by freshwater springs, adding to the trails' allure. Trail rides are limited to children over nine years of age. There is a weight limit as horses can only carry so much weight (see website below for details). They specialize in beginner and occasional riders, and most rides include a trot/jog pace, the slowest form of running in a horse. For children not of age, they offer pony rides as well. Be sure to dress for the weather in addition to wearing long pants even in the summer and appropriate shoes which are smooth soled and contain a prominent heel. They do not allow sneakers. However, they do loan out boots if needed.

http://www.deerpathstable.com/mobile/

Image by Margot O'Donnell

25. Fall Foliage Scenic Drive

Fall foliage peaks between mid-September and the end of October in Northeast Pennsylvania. The trees burst with glorious shades of oranges, yellows, and reds. While many hike to see these gorgeous colors, and I encourage you to, sometimes the best way to view them is by car. Since Pennsylvania typically boasts one of the longest fall foliage seasons on Earth, there is plenty of time to schedule your trip. You can check out the fall foliage reports through the DCNR website listed here: https://www.dcnr.pa.gov/

Conservation/ForestsAndTrees/FallFoliageReports/Pages/default.aspx

Listed as one of 7 eye-catching Poconos Fall Foliage Scenic Drives in the blog post listed below, the drive I will describe travels on route 209 through Monroe and Carbon Counties. This section of 209 skirts past Stroudsburg, then heads into the farmlands of Monroe and Carbon Counties. A detour onto Pohopoco drive will take you to Beltzville State Park to view the foliage reflected in the lake there. Don't miss stopping at the Country Junction, the World's Largest General Store in Lehighton that hosts the Great Pocono Pumpkin Festival each September through late October. Drive a few more miles to see the "Switzerland of America," picturesque Jim Thorpe.

https://www.poconomountains.com/blog/post/seven-eye-catching-fall-scenic-drives-in-the-poconos/

Image by Stockvault

Chapter Four

W **ayne County**

1. Wayne County Historical Society and Museum

810 Main St, Honesdale 18431 (570)253-3240

The Museum for the Wayne County Historical Society is home to a full-size replica of the Stourbridge Lion, a full-size replica of the first locomotive to run on a commercial track in the US. The Main Museum and Museum Shop are housed in an 1860s building that was the Delaware and Hudson Canal Company headquarters. The museum has four permanent exhibits:

- Movin' Energy: The History of the Delaware and Hudson Canal 1828-1898
- Faces in Clay
- Wayne County's Glass: Window Panes to White House Crystal
- Children's History Lab

Don't miss the Museum shop that sells historical books by Wayne County authors and many other Wayne County-related items.

https://www.waynehistorypa.com/museums/main

2. Pieces of the Past Antiques

518 twin rocks road (route 191) Newfoundland 18445 (845)392-5660

Pieces of the past is a fabulous antique store where you can get unique items at incredible prices. I got an antique armoire and a giant table for a steal- way less than you would pay in the city. Even with paying for a U-Haul to get it home to Philadelphia, it was still worth it. Pieces of the Past has been collecting items to fill their 5,700 square feet of showroom space, consisting of a barn and eight outbuildings, for 40+ years. Not only do they buy single items from customers, but they also buy entire estates. This means they truly have everything you can imagine. They have a wide selection of furniture, pottery, tools, toys, and clothes. The only negative about this place is that the outbuildings are not climate controlled, and items are often piled on top of each other. But if you're looking for something specific, like I was with the table and armoire, the owners know exactly where to look for it. And inside the barn showroom is climate controlled, and items are more thoughtfully laid out. Here, I found a dog cookie jar identical to the one I had as a child and in perfect condition again! If you have an antique or collectible, you can call or bring it in, and they may make you a cash offer on their spot for it. With new items being added weekly, it's an excellent place for a treasure hunt.

https://www.facebook.com/Pieces-of-the-past-584127055096817/

3. Lake Wallenpaupack

Lake Wallenpaupack is one of Pennsylvania's largest reservoirs, measuring 13 miles long with 52 miles of continuous shoreline. The area has numerous activities befitting its 5,700 acres of nature. The lake is bordered by the town of Hawley to the North and has many more local hubs, including Tafton, Paupack, Greentown, and Lakeville, all with fun activities. There are six public recreation areas to explore featuring hundreds of acres of forest lands, walking trails, campsites, and boat slips. Outfitters offer kayaks, water skiing, jet skis, wakeboarding, and boats to help pack in fun on the lake. Sunset is often visitors' favorite time of day on Lake Wallenpaupack, whether seen from the lake or the hiking trail. If you wish to view Sunset from the lake, I suggest booking a boat tour with **Wallenpaupack Scenic Boat Tours & Rentals**. They are located at 2487 Route 6 Hawley, PA (570)226-3293

They offer 50-minute boat tours where one can sit back and relax on their patio boats and enjoy the beautiful views of Lake Wallenpaupack while the tour guide describes the history behind the region. The tour covers approximately 1/3 of the lake. Or you can choose a two to three-hour charter trip on their Harris Sunliner pontoon boats. These excursions come with a Captain, tax, and gas included. Guests swim, have a tour, picnic, and enjoy the lake. Boat capacity is a minimum of four people maximum of 12. If your trip to Lake Wallenpaupack happens to be during the Fourth of July, you can also schedule a boat tour to watch the 4th of July fireworks on the lake. The boat departs at 8 p.m. and takes a short tour along the shoreline. Guests will learn the history of the lake as they spend time getting in the 4th of July spirit. The boat then docks close to the observation deck and dock to watch the fireworks display. Please note that the company only has boats with plastic resin chairs, and they do not have cushions, bug spray is recommended, and this trip is not handicap accessible. The journey is non-refundable. Unfortunately, pets are not allowed on any of these boat tours.

https://wallenpaupackboattour.com/tours/

If you're interested in local flora and fauna, visit Lacawac Sanctuary, which encompasses 550 Acres on the shores of Lake Wallenpaupack. The lake has many summertime water adventures, including swimming, jet skiing, and paddle boarding. You can rent jet skis from Lake Wallenpaupack boat rentals. See the website below for details.

https://www.paboatshop.com/lake-wallenpaupack-boat-rentals/

When winter arrives, Lake Wallenpaupack transforms into a winter wonderland. If you're in town at the beginning of February, don't miss the annual Wally IceFest. The ice fest consists of a two-day hockey tournament with live music, bonfires to keep you warm, ice golf, keg curling, keg tossing, ax throwing, etc. The event planners hope to have more than 30 teams hailing from Long Island, Philadelphia, Baltimore, and all points in between. Guests can enjoy drinks from local brewing companies and food from various vendors to round out the event.

During the rest of the winter on Lake Wallenpaupack, top outdoor activities include cross-country skiing, ice skating, snowshoeing, and ice fishing.

If you're a master angler or just a beginner, you can

borrow rods, reels, and a tackle box full of hooks and other necessary gear at the Lake Wallenpaupack Visitor Center.

https://www.poconomountains.com/blog/post/activi ties-to-do-around-lake-wallenpaupack/

4. Cross Current Guides Services and Outfitters

6048 Hancock Highway, Starlight 18461 (800)463-2750

Cross current Guides is an Orvis-endorsed fly fishing guide service located in New York and Pennsylvania's upper Delaware River system. They offer guided fly fishing for wild trout of the West, East, and Main stem of the Delaware River using drift boats, wading, or a combination of the two, depending on river conditions. They also guide on the storied waters of the Beaverkill, Willowemoc, and Neversink Rivers. The trout season begins in April and continues to late October for the Cross Current Guide Services. During the day, your skilled professional guides will help you spot fish and teach you techniques that will lead to the successful landing of fish. The guides will always have the right flies should you not be prepared with them, and loaner waders are also available depending on sizing. They are committed to doing everything to give you a fantastic day out on the river. All skill levels of anglers are welcome.

https://crosscurrentguideservice.com/

5. Golf

Cricket Hill Golf Club

176 Cricket Hill Rd, Hawley 18428 (570)226-4366

Cricket Golf Club offers beautiful scenic views and challenging play for golfers at every skill level. The course is well-groomed and allows for the best gameplay. The staff is available to offer tips and tricks so you can play your best round of golf. They're open seven days a week, weather permitting. You can choose to walk the course or rent a cart. The restaurant and bar, called Jiminy's, is open for dine-in or take-out and offers breakfast Friday, Saturday, and Sunday.

https://www.crickethillgc.com/

Image by Shawn Reza from Pixabay

6. D&H Trail

TRAIL END POINTS: Morse Ave., one block northwest of N. Main St./PA 171/Lackawanna River Heritage Trail (Simpson) and 0.5 miles north of Riverview Dr. and Damascus Road (Susquehanna)

The D&H Trail, also known as the Delaware and Hudson Rail Trail, is a moderately difficult hiking trail. It is 38.65 miles and spans three counties: Lackawanna, Susquehanna, and Wayne. The trail runs from the Simpson Viaduct at Route 171, off of Morse Avenue, North through Lanesboro to the New York state border, generally following the eastern edge of Susquehanna County. Towns include Simpson, Vandling, Forest City, Union Dale, Herrick Center, Burnwood, Ararat, Thompson, Starrucca, Stevens Point, and Lanesboro. Sixteen miles of the trail have been improved using stone dust suitable for hybrid and mountain bikes. Equestrians and Runners also use the trail in addition to hikers and bikers. The improved section of trail runs along the upper Lackawanna River from Vandling to Herrick Center to Ararat. Other sections of the D&H trail are graded with original rail bed surface suitable for mountain bikers and hikers.

https://www.traillink.com/trail/dh-rail-trail/
https://www.neparailtrails.org/guide/trails/

Image by Manfred Antranias Zimmer from Pixabay

7. Eagle Watch Bus Tours- Delaware Highlands Conservancy

Van Scott Nature Reserve 571 Perkins Pond Rd, Beach Lake 18405 (570) 226-3164

Hop on a heated bus and take a scenic drive through the Upper Delaware River region, looking for eagles in their natural habitats. Hosted by the Delaware Highlands Conservancy, you will be educated about eagles and their habitat during the journey. Your journey will start at the Van Scott Nature Reserve, located in Beach Lake, at the above address. Reservations are highly encouraged as seats are limited. It is recommended to dress warmly in layers and wear waterproof boots in addition to bringing binoculars, snacks, and a camera.

https://delawarehighlands.org/events/eagle-watch-bus-tours/2022-01-15/

Image by Mickey Estes from Pixabay

8. Jam Room Brewing Company

101 Creamery Rd, Greentown 18426 (570) 676-6070

The Jam Room Brewing Company started in 2010 when five lifelong friends decided to try something new. They repurposed their old music jam room into a room for brewing beer. They decided to open a brewery when they realized they had quite the knack for brewing great-tasting, all-natural beer. So in October of 2016, they opened the Jam Room Brewing Company. The Jam Room Brewing Company is where you can enjoy delicious tasting beer and listen to great music in a relaxed atmosphere. I love Jam room Brewery because their beer names have a musical theme. Beers such as Apple Records cider, Sabbath Black Stout, and Muddy Waters brown ale are some beers you can find at Jam Room Brewery. If you're not a big beer drinker, they also offer six different varieties of wines. Their gift shop also contains 64 Oz metal growlers, koozies, stickers, and t-shirts so that you can remember your time at Jam Room Brewery.

https://jamroombrewingco.wixsite.com/website

Image by Marcelo Ikeda Tchelão from Pixabay

9. D&H Canal Park at Lock 31 ✦ Towpath Trail

179 Texas Palmyra Hwy, Hawley 18428 (570) 253-3240

D&H in the D&H Canal Park stands for Delaware and Hudson. The D&H Canal is a 108 mi long achievement of civil engineering, built over three years, mainly by hand. The canal was created to transport anthracite coal from the Pennsylvania mines to the Hudson River in Kingston, New York, where it was shipped downriver to New York City. The 108 lock waterway operated from 1828 until 1898. The D&H Canal Park at Lock 31 spans 16 gorgeous acres and has much to explore. The site has the historic Daniels farmhouse built in the 1820s, the D&H canal, and Canal Lock 31. Many interpretive signs throughout the park give a brief history of the site. Walking along the towpath, you can find many local tree varieties, some of them quite rare. Also, keep an eye out for native wildlife species and the beautiful scenic views in the park. The park is open from dawn to dusk. There is a canal festival in August with living history demonstrations, guided tours, music, and vendors.

https://scenicwilddelawareriver.com/entries/d-h-canal-park-at-lock-31-hawley-pa/8e2acf8e-cc26-46f2-92fd-f44fdd85c749

10. Bethel School

294 Bethel School Rd, Honesdale 18431 (570) 253-3782

Bethel School is a perfectly preserved one-room schoolhouse built approximately in 1870 near the Pour Farm in Berlin Township. Everything in this schoolhouse is as it was when used, right down to the double wooden desks and textbooks from the era that remain on the bookcases. Bethel School closed in 1951 and has remained essentially unchanged since then. Wayne County was given a historic preservation award in 1998 for the restoration of the exterior of the schoolhouse. Since then, thousands of visitors have received valuable history lessons and had fun at Bethel School. Historical Society volunteers host free open houses and special spelling and geography bee programs. The school is available for group tours during warm weather months.

https://www.waynehistorypa.com/museums/bethelschool

11. The Settlers Inn

4 Main Ave, Hawley 18428 (570) 226-2993

The Settlers Inn, built in 1927, is a gorgeous example of English Arts and Crafts architecture. It was built shortly after Lake Wallenpaupack was created in 1925, thinking that tourism would come and those tourists would need a place to lodge. Unfortunately, World War II and the Great Depression forced the building to stay closed until 1944. The Settlers Inn has all the comforts of a bed and breakfast with the added convenience of an award-winning farm-to-table restaurant and tavern.

In addition, there are numerous outdoor adventures in the Delaware Highlands region to explore. The Settlers Inn sits on 6 acres of land with beautifully designed gardens bordered by the Lackawaxen River and woodlands containing a portion of the old Delaware and Hudson canal. When you visit Old Settlers Inn, I recommend having dinner at the farm-to-table restaurant run by chef Kate Woehrle. They are genuinely farm-to-table, sourcing ingredients from a small family farm in Wayne County. After dinner, spend time with your friends or family in the B&B's gorgeous common spaces. Relax on the terrace, stroll the colorful gardens, or take a trip down the meandering banks of the Lackawaxen River. If you're looking to be more active, borrow one of their bikes, and take a spin around town. You can also take a walk to Bingham Park and River-walk Trail and end up at their sister property, Ledges Hotel. Here you can relax on one of the many decks and surround yourself with the beauty of the waterfalls and the gorge. If unique dining is what you're looking for, book a spot in Grant's Woods. They have set up posh picnic tables, hammock chairs, a giant fire pit, an outdoor demonstration kitchen, and wicker furniture. It is located between the Inn's manicured gardens and the Lackawaxen River. The location, combined with strung-up party lights, gravel paths, and quaint cabins, creates a magical forest environment. Guests can enjoy an upscale picnic menu in a natural space.

The cabins feature glamorous decor such as chandeliers and antique furnishings to give the cabins a look of rustic elegance. The cabins are enclosed on three sides, with the back wall open to the beautiful Lackawaxen River.

The can't-miss event at the Old Settlers Inn is Jazz On the Deck. Jazz on the Deck has become a cherished rite of summer in the Poconos. The event draws professional performers with credits such as Broadway and the New York Cabaret scene. The event is held every Wednesday evening during the summer, and the lineup of musicians rotates. Guests can enjoy the farm-to-table Cuisine while overlooking the Inn's gorgeous Garden.

https://thesettlersinn.com/

12. Dorflinger Factory Museum

670 Texas Palmyra Hwy, Hawley 18428 (570)253-0220

The Dorflinger Factory Museum is a local industrial heritage museum celebrating the history and craftsmanship of the Dorflinger glass companies in Brooklyn, New York, and White Mills, Pennsylvania. The Dorflinger companies produced fine lead crystal tableware for U.S. Presidents, governments, and wealthy individuals during the Gilded Age in the United States. The factory contains a restored 1883 cutting shop and an 1888 factory office. With more than 2,600 finished glass objects, the Dorflinger glass collection at the Museum is one of the world's largest and most comprehensive collections of Dorflinger glass. The collection includes factory samples for orders for the White House, beginning with the Lincoln Administration and extending through the Wilson Administration. In addition to their extensive glass collection, the Dorflinger Factory Museum has a collection of artifacts from the White Mills

Factory, including glass blowing tools, benches, machinery, glass cutting and engraving equipment, and factory furniture. The museum also maintains a relatively extensive research library, including a collection of archival material that documents the years of operation of the Dorflinger factories in Brooklyn and White Mills and everyday life in the industrial village of White Mills. The Factory Museum was opened to the public in July 2016 following an extensive renovation of White Mills's two remaining factory buildings. These buildings are perfect examples of Pennsylvania Bluestone architecture. The interior of the factory building features woodwork from the Victorian era. There are several rules regarding photography in the factory museum. Photography must be conducted without disrupting the museum operation or blocking accessibility to entrances, exits, doorways, or high-traffic areas. Flash photography, the use of tripods, and the use of video or movie cameras are prohibited.

https://dorflingerfactorymuseum.com/

13. Dorflinger Suydam Wildlife Sanctuary

55 Suydam Dr, White Mills 18473 (570)253-1185

The sanctuary is home to the Dorflinger Glass Museum, dedicated to preserving the gorgeous glass made in White Mills from 1852 to 1921. The museum contains over nine hundred pieces of cut, engraved, etched, gilded, and enameled crystal that comprises the nation's most extensive collection of Dorflinger glass. The sanctuary is nearly 600 acres in area and contains miles of well-maintained walking trails popular among cross-country skiers in the winter. During the summer months in the sanctuary, the quiet is broken by the sounds of glorious music from

The Wildflower Music Festival. For more than 40 years, this festival has presented high-quality music in a natural amphitheater surrounded by majestic pines and sweet birdsong. Musicians playing at the festival represent a variety of musical styles, including classical, jazz, folk, bluegrass, and chamber repertoires. What better way to spend a Saturday evening than among the trees listening to great music while enjoying a picnic dinner and a glass of wine.

https://dorflinger.org/

14. Lacawac Sanctuary

94 Sanctuary Road, Lake Ariel 18436 (570)689-9494

Lacawac Sanctuary is dedicated to forging lifetime connections to the natural world and shaping the next generation of scientists and earth stewards through research, education, and preservation. Lacawac Sanctuary is a unique combination of an environmental education center, nature center, and biological field station. The sanctuary is nestled on 550 acres on the southern end of Lake Wallenpaupack. The sanctuary contains its own lake, Lake Lacawac, a glacial lake that is 13,000 years old and is the most pristine in the northern hemisphere because no motorized watercraft is ever allowed on the lake. Guests to the sanctuary will enjoy a rich outdoor education experience and exposure to diverse habitats, including wetlands, open fields, forests, and lakes. Lacawac is host to 9 miles of hiking trails open to the public, free of charge, and can be used from dawn to dusk year-round. You can hike to Lake Wallenpaupack or Lake Lacawac and everything in between. The sanctuary offers programs to the public, such as: Foraging in the Forest, where an experienced herbalist will take you for a walk around Lacawac looking for perennial vegetables, medicinal herbs, mushrooms, and forest edibles, Bird Walk at Lacawac, where experienced bird-watchers help you explore the area looking for birds setting up their nest as well as migrants passing through on their way further north, or Morning Paddle on Lake Lacawac where you will enjoy a morning on the lake after a short education on the ecological features of Lake Lacawac. An identification scavenger hunt is also available to interested participants in the program.

https://www.lacawac.org/

15. Audubon Art and Craft Festival

2552 US-6, Hawley 18428 (570) 226-4557

Suppose you're into art, especially nature and wildlife art, and seeing various wild animals up close. Why not visit the Audubon Art & Craft Festival held in the Wallenpau-pack Area High School gym every July. The Audubon Art & Craft Festival combines entertaining and educational live wildlife shows featuring native and exotic animals with close to 100 artists and artisans, many of whose work is nature or wildlife inspired. You can expect to find art forms such as painting, photography, and illustration with crafts including pottery, woodworking, glass work, wood carving, leatherwork, sheepskin, wheat weaving, metalworking, etc.

The animals will be shown by wildlife rehabilitators, expert bird and animal handlers, and wildlife educators who will present live shows featuring exotic and native animals and birds each day of the festival. When shows are not being held, the experts will be on the festival floor with the animals for the guests to view up close.

http://www.audubonfestival.com/

16. Maude Alley Shopping

1019-1023 Main Street, Honesdale 18431 (570) 642-1404

Maude Alley is a cute little "alley" on Main Street in downtown Honesdale that is formed by two buildings, one built-in 1845 and the other in 1880. The narrow alley not only contains six businesses but will lead you to a "secret garden."

One store I find particularly interesting is the **Mount Pleasant Herbary and Cafe** located at 1023 Main Street, Honesdale 18431 (570)229-6535.

Mount Pleasant Herbary was founded in 2009 by Gudrun Feigl, a native of Germany. After moving to the US in 2002, Gudrun desperately missed the wide selection of herbal tea blends from her home country, so she started to grow her own. That turned into making her own botanical soaps, salves, foot baths, and other herbal creations to add to her product line. In 2016 after selling her products at a local farmers market for seven years, Gudrun opened her first brick-and-mortar store in Honesdale on Maude Alley. Today, Mount Pleasant Herbary owns a 2-acre farm surrounded by wildflower meadows. They grow everything needed, except lavender, which is purchased from organic suppliers, to create their homemade products. They are also a European-style cafe featuring locally made baked goods from Sweet Cake Sensations in Hawley, including gluten-free and vegan options. They also offer a small lunch menu, including quiche, a variety of soups, and wraps. They serve their own organically-grown herbal tea blends served either hot or iced and French press coffee from local coffee roaster Black and Brass. They also offer workshops such as Lavender's Medicinal and Culinary Uses, Dandelion from Weed to Super Flower, Mint is Cooling, Beautiful Things to Make with Roses, Make a Natural First Aid Remedy Kit, and All About Elderberry.

https://www.facebook.com/visitmaudealley
https://www.mountpleasantherbary.com/

Image by gonghuimin468 from Pixabay

17. Old Stone Jail

Eastern end of Tenth Street, Honesdale, PA 18431 (570)253-3240 to arrange a private tour.

Take a tour of Wayne County's most fascinating historic site, the Old Stone Jail. The Old Stone Jail was built in 1859 and held Wayne County's criminals until 1935- a total of 76 years. The dank, bleak interiors were home to events like jailbreaks, hangings, and even the birth of a baby. The volunteer guides educate you on the jail's history and discuss some of the jail's most high-profile criminals. All of the stories told by the volunteers are gathered from local newspapers.

Check out the jail's Facebook page for up-to-date tour

information, or contact the historical society at the above number to schedule a private tour.

https://www.waynehistorypa.com/museums/oldstonejail

18. The Great Wall of Honesdale

110 4th St, Honesdale 18431

No, the Great Wall of Honesdale isn't a replica of the Great Wall of China. It's an outdoor art exhibition produced by the Wayne County Arts Alliance. Each year in May, new reproductions of original artwork are placed on the wall of a local building for art lovers to view from May through April, when they are replaced with new works of art. So, if you visit the Poconos yearly and anywhere near Honesdale, the Great Wall of Honesdale is worth checking out to see which artists they have chosen for this year.

http://www.thegreatwallofhonesdale.com/

19. Stourbridge Line

812 St, Honesdale 18431 (570)470-2697

4 Columbus Ave, Hawley 18428

Hop aboard a restored historic railroad coach and take any one of a variety of scenic or themed rides along the Lackawaxen River on the Stourbridge Line. The train departs either from the Honesdale or Hawley stations. All coaches are heated, and restrooms are available on the train and at the Honesdale station.

The Stourbridge Line is the place that saw the birthplace of America's first commercial railroad, with the Stourbridge Lion steam engine taking its inaugural trip here.

https://www.thestourbridgeline.net/

Image by Stockvault

20. Soaring Eagle Rail Tours

4 Columbus Ave, Hawley 18428 (570)229-2147

Railbiking is done on custom-made pedal-powered vehicles with four steel wheels, disc brakes, and pedals for each seat that glide effortlessly along railroad tracks. Because of the decreased friction between steel wheels and the steel tracks, pedaling the railbikes is relatively easy, making it ideal for the entire family. There is no need to steer, so you can spend more time watching wildlife found alongside the trails.

Soaring Eagle Rail Tours takes you on a scenic route that runs along the Lackawaxen River in the quaint town of Hawley. The trip is 6 miles and 2 hours long and is full of gorgeous views and fascinating history. Choose from either a tandem (two-seater) or a quad (four-seater) of their custom-made red, white, and blue railbikes. All guests ride simultaneously and are followed by a team of excellent tour guides placed in front and the back of the group, allowing friends and families to enjoy the experience together. The company recommends bringing the following items: a camera or smartphone, water, sunscreen, snacks, and bug spray. It is recommended to wear appropriate clothing based on the weather and for comfortability. Sturdy, closed-toe shoes are required. Athletic shoes are recommended. Not allowed are pets, drugs or alcohol of any kind, glass containers, sandals, flats, water socks, skirts (unless for religious observance), and music playing (for the courtesy of those around you).

Tours are run in rain or shine unless dangerous weather conditions occur. If cancellation due to weather occurs, a full refund will be issued.

There is a 300 lb weight limit per seat on the railbike, as anything over that weight runs the risk of the bike derailing. Children must be accompanied by a rider at least 16 years of age or older. Each guest must be secured in their seat with a seat belt, except infants, who must be secured to the chest of an adult rider using a harness. Children are not permitted to ride in the lap of an adult rider.

https://soarineagle.com/

21. Harmony In The Woods

19 Imagination Way, Hawley 18428 (570)588-8077

If you're a music-loving naturist or a nature-loving musicist...no, wait, that doesn't work, does it? Regardless, suppose you love nature and music. In that case, you will love Harmony In The Woods, an outdoor venue showcasing various blues, folk, bluegrass, jazz, Broadway, Celtic, country, funk, opera, comedy, and dance. The venue does not have permanent seating, but for the 2022 season, an outdoor folding chair will come with your tickets. You are also welcome to bring your own chair in addition to snacks and drinks. They ask that you not bring additional tables or other large items. If rain or disruptive weather occurs, the performance is held in a local church, usually Hawley United Methodist Church. Be advised that Harmony In The Woods is a non-smoking venue.

https://www.harmonyinthewoods.org/

22. Ritz Company Playhouse

512 Keystone St, Hawley 18428 (570)226-9752

Suppose you're in Hawley during the evening. Why not take in a performance at the Ritz Company Playhouse, a local Community Theater putting on live performances for over 49 years since June 29, 1973. The playhouse was once a vaudeville and movie theater. Their season opens in July and runs till September. You can catch a musical, a straight comedy, or a performance by their youngest actors in The Ritz Blitz group. They also put on a Christmas show during Hawley's Winterfest and several other events throughout the year. (see last entry for info on Hawley's Winterfest)

https://www.ritzplayhouse.com/

23. Penny Lane Candies and Candles

602 Church St, Hawley 18428 (570)226-1987

Craving candy? And candles? Head on down to Penny Lane Candies and Candles. You will be transported back to the Victorian era when you do. Penny Lane Candies and Candles is located in a gorgeous, restored 1890 Victorian building in Hawley. This family-run business offers over 500 varieties of candy, including hard-to-find candies that will send you down memory lane. They also have novelty candy and nearly 400 bins and barrels of various bulk candies that can be mixed and matched. They stock 50 flavors of Jelly Belly Ⓡ jelly beans, sugar-free candies, domestic and imported licorice, gigantic lollipops, and much more. So rev up that sweet tooth and schedule a visit.

In addition to candy, the store sells a variety of candles, gifts, metal signs, puzzles, hot sauces, vintage sodas, and more.

https://pennylanecandies.com/

24. Hawley Silk Mill

8 Silk Mill Drive, Hawley 18428 (570) 390-4440

The Silk Mill has been a part of the community on Hawley since it was built in 1880. Over the years, it has served as a silk factory, a textile factory, an antique center, and now a multipurpose building meant to celebrate the people of the Pocono Lake Region. A place for individuals to shop, gather, exercise, eat, and receive an education.

The Mill is the largest bluestone building globally at 75,000 square feet. The ground floor was designed by famous architect Peter Bohlin, who designed Apple retail stores. The sun streams into the retail spaces from the River Gorge behind the Mill through the many glass partitions dividing the spaces. Retail stores include a market and bakery containing specialty beers, several galleries, and various boutiques for clothes, shoes, antiques, and home accessories. The second floor is host to various professional offices, and the top floor contains Lackawanna Community College.

In front of the Mill is the small building that was once the storage facility for the silk cocoons for the Bellemonte Silk Mill (the former name of the Hawley Silk Mill). Now it is a specialty coffee house serving light meals and a place for people to gather and talk, aptly called The Cocoon. The Cocoon also has live entertainment along with the Boiler Room, which is located on the lower level of the Mill. There are weekly comedy shows and musical entertainment hosted by Harmony Presents.

https://hawleysilkmill.com/

25. Hawley Winterfest

If you're in the area for the Holiday season, make sure to stop in Hawley for their Winterfest. They festoon the town in twinkling lights with many fun holiday activities. Some of the previous years' Winterfest activities included horse-drawn carriage rides through town, snowman contests, tree decorating contests for charity, an arts and crafts fair, a beer tour, and a parade. Also offered are guided tours of 6 historic locations in the downtown Hawley area. A historical character will take you back in time by telling a piece of the town's history at each location. Even if you don't partake in any contests or tours, simply strolling down the streets and taking in the sights while listening to the holiday music filling the air is enough to put anyone into the holiday spirit.

https://visithawleypa.com/winterfest-home

Image by Jill Wellington from Pixabay

Afterword

As I said in the introduction, the Poconos are in my heart as one of my favorite places on the planet. The region has so much to offer, and the writing of this book opened my eyes to how much there truly is to do for every family member with various likes and dislikes in mind. I sincerely wish that you visit the Poconos and try one or two of these activities and fall in love with it as I have over my lifetime.

If you have enjoyed reading this book, please leave it a positive review on Amazon. Thank you, Lauren.

Thanks to my incredibly supportive husband, who helped me in countless ways as I wrote this book. He was my part-time photographer, editor, and head cheerleader while I created this comprehensive guide. I also want to thank my daughters for being patient, as I spent many hours writing and editing while they waited for me to be available. And, of course, my constant companion, sweet Kunu. He's my fourteen-year-old, 30-pound side-kick and was always there to offer furry comfort.

Kunu and I trout fishing at Buck Hill
Image by Lauren E Robins

About the Author

Lauren E Robins is a former veterinarian who has changed careers to author books and focus on charitable works. She runs an Etsy store selling hand-knitted items, with some proceeds going to charity. Since the age of nine, she has been knitting and enjoys spending time with her family. She has a loving, supportive husband, Seamus, two daughters, three cherished cats, and a beloved mutt, Kunu. Her favorite place to spend summers is in her house in Buck Hill Falls in the Poconos, which inspired her to write this book. Charitable gifts will be made with a percentage of the author's publishing proceeds.

 facebook.com/laurenschneiderrobins

 instagram.com/lerdvmo6

 tiktok.com/@lrobinswithoneb

Citations

Citations

Great Wolf Lodge. (n.d.). Indoor Water Park & Resort | Poconos Resort | Great Wolf Lodge. Retrieved May 21, 2022, from https://www.great wolf.com/poconos

Quiet Valley Living Historical Farm. (2022). Quiet Valley Living Historical Farm. Retrieved May 22, 2022, from https://quietvalley.org/

Frazetta Art Museum. (2022). Frazetta Art Museum. Retrieved May 22, 2022, from http://www.frazettamuseum.com

Antoine Dutot Museum & Gallery. (2021). Antoine Dutot Museum & Gallery. Retrieved May 22, 2022, from http://www.dutotmuseum.com

Antoine Dutot Museum & Gallery - Delaware Water Gap, PA | Scenic Wild Delaware River. (2022). Antoine Dutot Museum & Gallery - Delaware Water Gap, PA. Retrieved May 22, 2022, from https://scenicwild-delawareriver.com/entries/antoine-dutot-museum-gallery-delaware-water-gap-pa/a1073a9a-c3e8-4d11-b858-23d9bc42abed

Pocono Raceway. (2022, May 24). Pocono Raceway - The Tricky Triangle. Retrieved May 22, 2022, from https://www.poconoraceway.com/

Pocono Raceway. (n.d.). Academic Dictionaries and Encyclopedias. Retrieved May 22, 2022, from https://en-academic.com/dic.nsf/enwiki/362529

Elements Music & Arts Festival. (n.d.). Elements Festival. Retrieved May 22, 2022, from https://www.elementsfest.us/#

Callie's Candy Kitchen. (2020). Callie's Candy Kitchen. Retrieved May 22, 2022, from https://www.calliescandy.com

Harry D. Callie. (2020, April 23). Candy Hall of Fame. Retrieved May 22, 2022, from https://candyhalloffame.org/inductee/harry-d-callie/#:%7E:text=Harry%20passed%20away%20October%2024%2C%202013.

Delaware Water Gap National Recreation Area (U.S. National Park Service). (n.d.). National Park Service. Retrieved May 22, 2022, from https://www.nps.gov/dewa/index.htm

Eating & Sleeping - Delaware Water Gap National Recreation Area (U.S. National Park Service). (n.d.). National Park Service. Retrieved May 22, 2022, from https://www.nps.gov/dewa/planyourvisit/eatingsleep ing.htm

Citations

Picnic - Delaware Water Gap National Recreation Area (U.S. National Park Service). (n.d.). National Park Service. Retrieved May 22, 2022, from https://www.nps.gov/dewa/planyourvisit/picnic.htm

Hiking - Delaware Water Gap National Recreation Area (U.S. National Park Service). (n.d.). National Park Service. Retrieved May 22, 2022, from https://www.nps.gov/dewa/planyourvisit/trails.htm

Historic Places - Delaware Water Gap National Recreation Area (U.S. National Park Service). (n.d.). National Park Service. Retrieved May 22, 2022, from https://www.nps.gov/dewa/planyourvisit/historic-places.htm

Raymondskill Creek Trail - Delaware Water Gap National Recreation Area (U.S. National Park Service). (n.d.). National Park Service. Retrieved May 22, 2022, from https://www.nps.gov/dewa/planyourvisit/raymondskill-creek-trail.htm

Silverthread Falls. (2019, May 18). Great Lakes Waterfalls & Beyond. Retrieved May 22, 2022, from http://gowaterfalling.com/waterfalls/silverthread.shtml

Dingmans Creek Trail - Delaware Water Gap National Recreation Area (U.S. National Park Service). (n.d.). National Park Service. Retrieved May 22, 2022, from https://www.nps.gov/dewa/planyourvisit/dingmans-creek-trail.htm

Visitor Centers - Delaware Water Gap National Recreation Area (U.S. National Park Service). (n.d.). National Park Service. Retrieved May 22, 2022, from https://www.nps.gov/dewa/planyourvisit/visitorcenters.htm

Aquatopia | Poconos Indoor Waterpark Resort | PA's #1 Indoor Waterpark. (2022, May 6). Camelback. Retrieved May 22, 2022, from https://www.camelbackresort.com/waterparks/poconos-pa-indoor-water-park/

Outdoor Waterpark in Poconos PA | Camelbeach. (2022, May 26). Camelback. Retrieved May 22, 2022, from https://www.camelbackresort.com/waterparks/poconos-pa-outdoor-water-park/

Kalahari Resorts & Conventions. (n.d.). Kalahari. Retrieved May 22, 2022, from https://www.kalahariresorts.com/pennsylvania/

N. (2022, May 26). Mountain Resort in Pennsylvania. Mount Airy Casino Resort. Retrieved May 22, 2022, from https://mountairycasino.com/

Pocono Mountains Music Festival. (n.d.). PoconoFest. Retrieved May 22, 2022, from https://www.poconofest.org/

Paradise Brook Trout Co. - Quality Since 1901. (2022, March 21). Paradise Brook Trout Co. Retrieved May 23, 2022, from https://paradisetrout.com/

Big Brown Fish & Pay Lakes - Where the Fish are Always Biting! (2022,

May 27). Big Brown Fish & Pay Lakes. Retrieved May 23, 2022, from https://bigbrownfish.com/

C. (2020, February 10). Austin T. Blakeslee Natural Area. Brodhead Watershed Association. Retrieved May 23, 2022, from https://brodheadwatershed.org/austin-t-blakeslee-natural-area/

Falls, B. H. (n.d.). Buck Hill Falls Golf Club. Buck Hill Falls. Retrieved May 23, 2022, from https://www.buckhillfalls.com/public/golf

Poconos Golf Courses at Shawnee Inn: Packages & Getaways. (2022, May 18). Shawnee Inn. Retrieved May 23, 2022, from https://www.shawneeinn.com/poconos-golf-courses/

Mountain Creek Riding Stables. (2022, May 6). Horseback Riding in the Poconos, PA: Retrieved May 23, 2022, from https://mtcreekstable.com/

Adventure Sports. (n.d.). Adventure Sports. Retrieved May 23, 2022, from https://www.adventuresport.com

DCNR. (n.d.). Big Pocono State Park. Pennsylvania Department of Conservation & Natural Resources. Retrieved May 24, 2022, from https://www.dcnr.pa.gov/StateParks/FindAPark/BigPoconoState-Park/Pages/default.aspx

Pocono Go. (2021, December 22). Big Pocono State Park. PoconoGo. Retrieved May 24, 2022, from https://poconogo.com/park-preserve/big-pocono-state-park/

Stroud Mansion | Monroe County Historical Association. (n.d.). Monroe County Historical Association. Retrieved May 25, 2022, from https://www.monroehistorical.org/mansion.html

Visit Downtown Stroudsburg Pennsylvania. (n.d.). Visit Downtown Stroudsburg. Retrieved May 25, 2022, from https://www.visitdowntown-stroudsburg.com/

Cherry Valley National Wildlife Refuge. (n.d.). U.S. Fish and Wildlife Service. Retrieved May 25, 2022, from https://www.fws.gov/refuge/cherry-valley

Pocono Peddler's Village Antique Mall. (n.d.). Pocono Peddler's Village Antique Mall. Retrieved May 25, 2022, from https://pocono-antique-mall.com/

Olde Engine Works Antique Marketplace. (n.d.). Olde Engine Works. Retrieved May 25, 2022, from https://www.oldeengineworks.com/

Backroads Antiques | Henryville. (2020, July 16). DiscoverNEPA. Retrieved May 25, 2022, from https://www.discovernepa.com/thing-to-do/backroads-antiques/

Barn Door Antiques. (n.d.). Barn Door Antiques. Retrieved May 25, 2022, from http://www.barndoorantiques.com/

Citations

Ski & Snowboard Ticket Deals on Sale Now! (n.d.). Blue Mountain Resort. Retrieved May 25, 2022, from https://www.skibluemt.com/

Camelback Resort | Pocono Mountain Resort | Family Resort in Poconos PA. (2022, June 2). Camelback. Retrieved May 25, 2022, from https://www.camelbackresort.com/

L. (2021, October 28). The Mountain. Shawnee Mountain Ski Area. Retrieved May 25, 2022, from https://www.shawneemt.com/mountain/

Skytop Lodge. (2022, June 1). Skytop Lodge | Luxury Poconos Resort | Skytop, PA. Retrieved May 25, 2022, from https://www.skytop.com/

Simon Property Group, L.P. and/or Its Affiliates (NYSE: SPG), © Copyright 1999–2022. All Rights Reserved. (n.d.). The Crossings Premium Outlets. Simon Premium Outlets. Retrieved May 25, 2022, from https://www.premiumoutlets.com/bot-challenge?url=L291dGxldC90a-GUtY3Jvc3NpbmdzPw==&uuid=8cb83a4a-e2eb-11ec-ad1b-4a537476624c&vid=

Arctic Paws Sled Dog Tours. (n.d.). Arctic Paws Dog Sled Tours. Retrieved May 25, 2022, from https://www.arcticpawsdogsledtours.com/

Home - Moyer Aviation. (n.d.). Moyer Aviation Incorporated. Retrieved May 25, 2022, from http://moyeraviation.com/

Sorrenti Family Estate. (n.d.). Sorrenti. Retrieved May 25, 2022, from https://www.sorrentifamilyestate.com/

Klues – Escape Room – www.klues.com. (n.d.). Klues Escape Room. Retrieved June 3, 2022, from https://klues.com/

Schisler Museum & McMunn Planetarium. (n.d.). East Stroudsburg University. Retrieved May 25, 2022, from https://www.esu.edu/museum/index.cfm

C. (2022a, May 13). 8 Pennsylvania Swimming Holes That Will Make Your Summer Memorable. OnlyInYourState. Retrieved May 25, 2022, from https://www.onlyinyourstate.com/pennsylvania/pa-swimming-holes/

Hackers Trail - Delaware Water Gap National Recreation Area (U.S. National Park Service). (n.d.). National Park Service. Retrieved May 25, 2022, from https://www.nps.gov/dewa/planyourvisit/hackers-trail.htm

Costa's Family Fun Park. (n.d.). Costa"s Family Fun Park. Retrieved May 25, 2022, from https://www.costasfamilyfunpark.com

Bushkill Falls | The Niagara of Pennsylvania. (n.d.). BushkillFalls. Retrieved May 25, 2022, from https://www.visitbushkillfalls.com/

Woodloch Resort | All-Inclusive Family Resorts - Best Poconos Resorts. (2022, May 23). Woodloch Resort. Retrieved May 25, 2022, from https://www.woodloch.com/

The Lodge at Woodloch | Spa Resorts in PA | Official Site. (n.d.). The Lodge at Woodloch. Retrieved May 25, 2022, from https://www.thelodgeatwoodloch.com/

Grey Towers Heritage Association. (2022, May 20). Grey Towers Heritage Association. Retrieved May 26, 2022, from https://greytowers.org/

N. (2022b, April 7). Official. Milford Tourism & Visitor Information. Milford Presents. Retrieved May 26, 2022, from https://milfordpa.us/

K. (2022b, March 1). At The Columns. Pike County Historical Society. Retrieved May 26, 2022, from http://pikehistorical.org/

Fishing - Upper Delaware Scenic & Recreational River (U.S. National Park Service). (n.d.). National Park Service. Retrieved May 26, 2022, from https://www.nps.gov/upde/planyourvisit/fishing.htm

Waterwheel Café, Bakery & Bar. (2021, October 8). Upper Mill Grist Mill Milford PA Pike County PA Restaurant. Waterwheel Cafe, Bakery and Bar Milford PA 18337. Retrieved May 26, 2022, from https://www.waterwheelcafe.com/upper-mill-grist-mill-milford-pa-pike-county-pa-restaurant/

Paupack Hills A Pocono Mountains Destination. (2014). Paupack Hills. Retrieved May 26, 2022, from http://paupackhills.com/

Zane Grey - Upper Delaware Scenic & Recreational River (U.S. National Park Service). (n.d.). National Park Service. Retrieved May 26, 2022, from https://www.nps.gov/upde/learn/historyculture/zanegrey.htm

Pocono Environmental Education Center. (2012, August 23). PEEC. Retrieved May 26, 2022, from https://www.peec.org/

Eagle Watching in Lackawaxen Attraction Details. (n.d.). Explore PA History. Retrieved May 26, 2022, from http://explorepahistory.com/attraction.php?id=1-B-2C35

Eagle Observation Blind Map. (n.d.). [Map]. Delaware Highlands. https://delawarehighlands.org/wp-content/uploads/eagle_observation_blind-map.pdf

Lower Hornbecks Creek Trail - Delaware Water Gap National Recreation Area (U.S. National Park Service). (n.d.). National Park Service. Retrieved May 26, 2022, from https://www.nps.gov/dewa/planyourvisit/hornbecks-creek-trail.htm

Delaware River rafting, tubing, canoeing and kayaking - Indian Head Canoes. (2022, April 15). Indian Head. Retrieved May 26, 2022, from https://www.indianheadcanoes.com/

Ski Big Bear. (n.d.). Ski Big Bear. Retrieved May 26, 2022, from https://www.ski-bigbear.com/

Gallery | Artery Gallery | Milford. (n.d.). Artery Gallery. Retrieved June 3, 2022, from https://www.arterygallerymilford.com/

Raymondskill Creek Trail - Delaware Water Gap National Recreation Area (U.S. National Park Service). (n.d.-b). National Park Service. Retrieved

May 26, 2022, from https://www.nps.gov/dewa/planyourvisit/ray-mondskill-creek-trail.htm

Roebling's Delaware Aqueduct (Roebling Bridge) - Upper Delaware, PA/NY | Scenic Wild Delaware River. (n.d.). National Geographic. Retrieved May 26, 2022, from https://scenicwilddelawareriver.com/en-tries/roeblings-delaware-aqueduct-roebling-bridge-upper-delaware-pa-ny/93c62f22-f38d-42f9-b4d5-8ceof83e9f3f

Keough, J. (2022, June 2). Kittatinny Canoes- Matamoros Base. Kittatinny Canoes. Retrieved May 26, 2022, from https://kittatinny.com/direc-tions/matamoras-base/

Shohola Falls | Shohola, PA 18458. (n.d.). Pocono Mountains Visitors Bureau. Retrieved May 26, 2022, from https://www.poconomountains.-com/listing/shohola-falls/1680/

Swim - Delaware Water Gap National Recreation Area (U.S. National Park Service). (n.d.). National Park Service. Retrieved May 26, 2022, from https://www.nps.gov/dewa/planyourvisit/swim.htm

Dingmans Creek Trail - Delaware Water Gap National Recreation Area (U.S. National Park Service). (n.d.-b). National Park Service. Retrieved May 27, 2022, from https://www.nps.gov/dewa/planyourvisit/ding-mans-creek-trail.htm

Milford Beach. (n.d.). Outdoor Project. Retrieved May 27, 2022, from https://www.outdoorproject.com/united-states/pennsylvania/milford-beach

Log Tavern Brewing Company | Milford P.A. | Log Tavern Brewing. (n.d.). Logtavernbrewing. Retrieved May 27, 2022, from https://www.logtav-ernbrewing.com/

HOME | The Artisan Exchange, Milford, PA. Gallery of American Gifts and Fine Art. (n.d.). Artisanexchange. Retrieved May 27, 2022, from https://www.theartisanexchange.com/

Eckley Miners Village Museum. (n.d.). Eckleyminersvillage. Retrieved May 27, 2022, from http://eckleyminersvillage.com/

Lehigh Gorge Scenic Railroad. (n.d.). Lehighgorgescenicrailroad. Retrieved May 27, 2022, from https://www.lgsry.com/

Little Gap Covered Bridge. (n.d.). Wikiwand. Retrieved May 27, 2022, from https://www.wikiwand.com/en/Little_Gap_Covered_Bridge

National Park Service. (1980). Covered Bridges of the Delaware River. PennDot. https://gis.penndot.gov/CRGISAttachments/SiteResource/H001306_01H.pdf

Wikipedia contributors. (2022, May 7). Howe truss. Wikipedia. Retrieved May 27, 2022, from https://en.wikipedia.org/wiki/Howe_truss

Cheney, J. (2021, November 14). Visiting the Covered Bridges in Carbon

Citations

County, PA. Uncovering PA. Retrieved May 27, 2022, from https://uncoveringpa.com/visiting-the-covered-bridges-in-carbon-county-pa

Oktoberfest 2021. (n.d.). Blue Mountain Resort. Retrieved May 27, 2022, from https://www.skibluemt.com/upcoming-events/oktoberfest

Jack Frost Big Boulder | Jack Frost Big Boulder Resort. (n.d.). Jfbb. Retrieved May 27, 2022, from https://www.jfbb.com/

Mauch Chunk Lake Park. (n.d.). Carbon County. Retrieved May 28, 2022, from https://www.carboncounty.com/index.php/park

Francis E. Walter Dam. (n.d.). Recreation.Gov. Retrieved May 28, 2022, from https://www.recreation.gov/camping/gateways/198

Welcome to Francis E Walter Dam and Reservoir. (n.d.). US Army Corps of Engineers. Retrieved May 28, 2022, from https://www.nap.usace.army.mil/Missions/Civil-Works/Francis-E-Walter-Dam/

Mauch Chunk Lake Park | Jim Thorpe. (2021, November 15). Discover-NEPA. Retrieved May 28, 2022, from https://www.discovernepa.com/thing-to-do/mauch-chunk-lake-park/

Penn's Peak. (n.d.). Penn's Peak. Retrieved May 28, 2022, from https://www.pennspeak.com/

Manor, T. F. (2022, March 7). Here's Why You Need to Visit Penn's Peak in the Poconos. The French Manor Inn and Spa. Retrieved May 28, 2022, from https://thefrenchmanor.com/blog/penns-peak-poconos/#:%7E:text=No%20matter%20which%20seat%20you,the%20most%20breathtaking%20mountain%20views.

DCNR. (n.d.-a). Beltzville State Park. Pennsylvania Department of Conservation & Natural Resources. Retrieved May 28, 2022, from https://www.dcnr.pa.gov/StateParks/FindAPark/BeltzvilleStatePark/Pages/default.aspx

DCNR. (n.d.-c). Lehigh Gorge State Park. Pennsylvania Department of Conservation & Natural Resources. Retrieved May 29, 2022, from https://www.dcnr.pa.gov/StateParks/FindAPark/LehighGorgeStatePark/Pages/default.aspx

Whitewater Challengers. (2022, May 23). Lehigh River â Poconos, PA - Whitewater Challengers. Retrieved May 29, 2022, from https://whitewaterchallengers.com/locations/lehigh-river-poconos-pa/

Visit Victorian Splendor! The Asa Packer Mansion Museum in Jim Thorpe! (n.d.). Asa Packer Mansion Museum. Retrieved May 29, 2022, from http://www.asapackermansion.com/

Old Jail Museum. (n.d.). Old Jail Museum. Retrieved May 29, 2022, from http://www.theoldjailmuseum.com/

Bear Mountain Butterfly Sanctuary. (2022, April 11). Bear Mountain Butterfly Sanctuary in the Pocono Mountains. Retrieved May 30, 2022, from https://bearmountainbutterflies.com/

Mauch Chunk Opera House. (n.d.). Mauch Chunk Opera House. Retrieved May 30, 2022, from https://mcohjt.com/

MCMMC – Jim Thorpe Museum. (n.d.). Mauch Chunk Museum and Cultural Center. Retrieved May 30, 2022, from https://mauchchunkmcc.org/

Pocono Whitewater. (n.d.). Pocono Whitewater. Retrieved May 30, 2022, from https://www.poconowhitewater.com

Pocono Biking. (2022, February 2). Pocono Biking: Pocono Bike Trails | Pocono Outdoor Adventures | Biking. Retrieved May 30, 2022, from https://poconobiking.com/

Skirmish Paintball. (2022, April 20). Skirmish Paintball: Pocono Paintball Facility | Best Paintball Fields. Skirmish. Retrieved May 30, 2022, from https://www.skirmish.com/

Jim Thorpe Sidecar Tourz. (n.d.). Jim Thorpe Sidecar Tourz. Retrieved May 30, 2022, from https://www.jimthorpesidecartourz.com/

Welcome to the Broadway Grille and Pub. (n.d.). Broadway Grille. Retrieved May 31, 2022, from https://broadwaygrillepub.com/

S. (n.d.). The Stabin Museum. The Stabin Museum. Retrieved May 31, 2022, from http://stabinmuseum.com/

No. 9 Coal Mine. (n.d.). No. 9 Coal Mine. Retrieved May 31, 2022, from https://no9minemuseum.wixsite.com/museum

Welcome To Deerpath Stable. (n.d.). Deerpath Stable. Retrieved May 31, 2022, from http://www.deerpathstable.com/mobile/

Fall Foliage | Endless Mountains Heritage Region. (n.d.). Endless Mountains Heritage Region. Retrieved May 31, 2022, from https://www.emheritage.org/fall-foliage/?gclid=CjoKCQjw-daUBh-CIARIsALbkjSaoVcCFkGQqZhyKvmyuoBor17egb-caAa6ncck1YfN-L7jNR2oESm3IaAnKoEALw_wcB

Whalen, E. (2021, September 29). 7 Eye-Catching Poconos Fall Foliage Scenic Drives. Pocono Mountains Visitors Bureau. Retrieved May 31, 2022, from https://www.poconomountains.com/blog/post/seven-eye-catching-fall-scenic-drives-in-the-poconos/

Main Museum :: Wayne County Historical Society. (n.d.). Wayne County Historical Society. Retrieved May 31, 2022, from https://www.wayne-historypa.com/museums/main

Staff, A. T. (2020, July 1). Pieces of the Past. Antique Trader. Retrieved May 31, 2022, from https://www.antiquetrader.com/directory-antique-businesses/pieces-of-the-past

Pieces of the Past | Newfoundland. (2021, April 15). DiscoverNEPA.

Retrieved May 31, 2022, from https://www.discovernepa.com/thing-to-do/pieces-of-the-past/

Facebook - Pieces of the Past. (n.d.). Facebook. Retrieved May 31, 2022, from https://www.facebook.com/Pieces-of-the-past-584127055096817/

The Boat Shop. (2021, December 21). Boat Shop | Lake Wallenpaupack Boat Rentals. Retrieved May 31, 2022, from https://www.paboatshop.com/lake-wallenpaupack-boat-rentals/

Whalen, E. (2022, March 29). 8 Activities to Do around Lake Wallenpaupack. Pocono Mountains Visitors Bureau. Retrieved May 31, 2022, from https://www.poconomountains.com/blog/post/activities-to-do-around-lake-wallenpaupack/

Wallenpaupack Boat Tours. (2021, December 23). Lake Wallenpaupack Scenic Boat Tours. Retrieved May 31, 2022, from https://wallenpaupackboattour.com/tours/

Cross Current – Guide Service & Outfitters. (n.d.). Cross Current Guide Service and Outfitters. Retrieved May 31, 2022, from https://crosscurrentguideservice.com/

D&H Rail Trail. (n.d.). Trail Link. Retrieved May 31, 2022, from https://www.traillink.com/trail/dh-rail-trail/

TRAILS | NEPA Rail Trails. (n.d.). Rail Trail Council of NEPA. Retrieved May 31, 2022, from https://www.neparailtrails.org/guide/trails/

Cricket Hill Golf Club. (n.d.). Cricket Hill Golf Club. Retrieved May 31, 2022, from https://www.crickethillgc.com/

Eagle Watch Bus Tours – Delaware Highlands Conservancy. (n.d.). Delaware Highlands Conservancy. Retrieved June 1, 2022, from https://delawarehighlands.org/events/eagle-watch-bus-tours/2022-01-15/

Jam Room Brewing Company. (n.d.). Jam Room Brewing Company. Retrieved June 1, 2022, from https://jamroombrewingco.wixsite.com/website

D & H Canal Park at Lock 31 - Hawley, PA | Scenic Wild Delaware River. (n.d.). National Geographic. Retrieved June 1, 2022, from https://scenicwilddelawareriver.com/entries/d-h-canal-park-at-lock-31-hawley-pa/8e2acf8e-cc26-46f2-92fd-f44fdd85c749

D&H Canal Park at Lock 31 | Hawley. (2022, February 10). DiscoverNEPA. Retrieved June 1, 2022, from https://www.discovernepa.com/thing-to-do/dh-canal-park-at-lock-31/

Bethel School :: Wayne County Historical Society. (n.d.). Wayne County Historical Society. Retrieved June 1, 2022, from https://www.waynehistorypa.com/museums/bethelschool

Citations

Poconos Bed and Breakfast | Hawley PA Bed and Breakfast | The Settlers Inn. (2022, May 23). Thesettlersinn. Retrieved June 1, 2022, from https://thesettlersinn.com/

Historical Dorflinger Glass Factory Museum in White Mills PA & Brooklyn NY. (2021, September 3). Dorflinger Factory Museum. Retrieved June 1, 2022, from https://dorflingerfactorymuseum.com/

Dorflinger-Suydam. (2021, October 6). Dorflinger-Suydam - Wildlife Sanctuary . Glass Museum . Wildflower Music Festival . Historic White Mills. Retrieved June 1, 2022, from https://dorflinger.org/

Lacawac Sanctuary. (n.d.). Lacawac Sanctuary Field Station. Retrieved June 1, 2022, from https://www.lacawac.org

C., C., & C. (n.d.-a). Audubon Art and Craft Festival. Audubon Art and Craft Festival, Hawley, PA. Retrieved June 1, 2022, from http://www.audubonfestival.com/

Maude Alley | Honesdale PA Unique Shops | 570-642-1404 | Poconos Shopping |. (n.d.). Commissioners of Wayne County. Retrieved June 1, 2022, from http://www.visitwaynecounty.com/place/Maude_Alley

Visit Maude Alley. (n.d.). Facebook. Retrieved June 1, 2022, from https://www.facebook.com/visitmaudealley

Gift Shop Mount Pleasant Herbary Honesdale PA. (n.d.). Mountpleasantherbary. Retrieved June 1, 2022, from https://www.mountpleasantherbary.com/

Old Stone Jail :: Wayne County Historical Society. (n.d.). Wayne County Historical Society. Retrieved June 2, 2022, from https://www.waynehistorypa.com/museums/oldstonejail

The Great Wall of Honesdale. (n.d.). The Great Wall of Honesdale. Retrieved June 2, 2022, from http://www.thegreatwallofhonesdale.com

The Stourbridge Line - Honesdale PA Train Ride! (n.d.). THE STOURBRIDGE LINE. Retrieved June 2, 2022, from https://www.thestourbridgeline.net/

Scenic and Recreational Railbiking Adventure. (n.d.). Soarin' Eagle Rail Tours. Retrieved June 2, 2022, from https://soarineagle.com

Capistrant, J. (2021, March 17). The First and Only Rail Bike Experience in Pennsylvania: Colebrookdale's Secret Valley Rail Bike Explorers. Phoenixville Chamber of Commerce. Retrieved June 2, 2022, from https://phoenixvillechamber.org/news-events/news/the-first-and-only-rail-bike-experience-in-pennsylvania-colebrookdales-secret-valley-rail-bike-explorers/

Harmony In The Woods | Outdoor Concert Theater in Hawley, PA. (2022, May 17). Harmony In The Woods. Retrieved June 2, 2022, from https://www.harmonyinthewoods.org/

166

Citations

Ritz Company Playhouse. (n.d.). Ritz Playhouse. Retrieved June 2, 2022, from https://www.ritzplayhouse.com/

Welcome to Penny Lane Candy and Candles. (n.d.). Penny Lane Candy and Candles. Retrieved June 2, 2022, from https://pennylanecandies.com

Welcome to the Hawley Silk Mill. (2021, March 26). Hawley Silk Mill. Retrieved June 2, 2022, from https://hawleysilkmill.com/

Winterfest Home. (n.d.). Downtown Hawley Partnership. Retrieved June 2, 2022, from https://visithawleypa.com/winterfest-home

Made in the USA
Columbia, SC
29 September 2023

23613063R00102